MW00354422

# UNVEILING
# **THE MODERN**
# *GODDESS*

## Thru Symbolism,
## Chakras & Myth

*And,*
*wishing you much love*
*& blessings or your journey.*

*Karen Marie Castle*

Unveiling the Modern Goddess: Thru Symbolism, Chakras & Myth.

Copyright © 2011 Karen M Castle. All rights reserved.

*All rights reserved under copyright laws. Printed in the United States of America. No part of this book may be used or reproduced in any manner whatsoever without written permission except in the case of brief quotations embodied in critical articles and reviews.*

First Edition. Printed in the United States by Instant Publishers.

The author has made every effort to trace copyright owners. Where she has failed, she offers her apologies and undertakes to make proper acknowledgement where possible in reprints.

Cover Design by Camille Charles of Chamillah Designs
http://www.chamillah.com

ISBN: 978-0-578-08417-6

Library of Congress Cataloging-in-Publication Data
Case File 1-604821901

Castle, Karen M.    •

    Unveiling the modern goddess: thru symbolism, chakras & myth

    Transpersonal psychology, self-growth, healing medicine.

To contact the author to propose workshops or lectures, email info@karencastle.com.

*FOR MY MOM,
MY FRIEND & CONFIDANT,
THANK YOU FOR YOUR
LOVE & SUPPORT*

# TABLE OF CONTENTS

# ACKNOWLEDGMENTS

*My gratitude goes out to all those who supported me and believed in me through this process.*

*I want to thank my son, Clint, for being my teacher in so many ways—most especially, for my depth of knowing and experiencing unconditional love.*

*For my husband Peter, thank you for your love and for listening with eager ears as I shared my ideas with you. Thank you for your support and wisdom.*

*Thank you to my family for your encouragement and your open mind even when you may not understand exactly what it is I do.*

*To my dear friend and confidant, Jane, thank you for being my 'Ninshubur'. I have always appreciated your wisdom. You are a blessing in my life.*

*Thank you to Joan Sheehan for helping me through the original, unedited version. Thank you to Kerry as well, for your willingness to stay objective and provide solid edits.*

*A big thanks to Camille for your patience in collaborating with me on the cover design.*

*Lastly, I want to thank all my teachers, those in spirit and those in this realm.*

# Foreword

*This book developed out of a connection with a Divine presence. While writing it, I often felt the words came through me as well as the ideas. At times, I didn't understand where I was going with it and it felt like it had a life of its own. At the end, it clicked; the seven areas of woman's life can be looked at as a simple outline.*

*Chapter Two - Women Nurturing and Caring*
*Chapter Three - Women Owning Their Feminine Virtues*
*Chapter Four - Women Empowered*
*Chapter Five - Women and Love*
*Chapter Six - Women Taking Responsibility*
*Chapter Seven - Women Visionaries*
*Chapter Eight - Women Crowned*

*This is the time for women to embrace their full power. Women are being called to step up and take responsibility for their lives and the lives of their families. This is not about "fixing" people, this is about ownership. Taking full responsibility means owning our shadow and recognizing behaviors that are detrimental to humanity's future growth. It also means owning our ability to make changes and be transformed through the process. Our world is going through a unique transformation right now. We need all the help we can get to assist with the upcoming conversion of masculine and feminine energy.*

*If nothing else, remember that we are all loved. Some of us will not make it through the transformation, it will be too difficult. Some of us will guide the way. Whatever you are called to do, be present with it and with grace and ease, the Goddess will bless you in all your ways.*

# Introduction –
# A Spiritual Quest

*The most beautiful experience we can have*
*is the mysterious...*
*He to whom this emotion is a stranger,*
*who can no longer pause to wonder*
*and stand rapt in awe,*
*is as good as dead.*
*~Albert Einstein*

Something shifted for me in the new millennia and the
year 2000. It was subtle at the time but I would now call it
my spiritual quest. It seems strange even to call it that. I
didn't know what I was searching for but I knew that I felt
a deep inner stir. I obviously already had a spiritual thirst.
I went to church every week, sometimes everyday, but
what I was searching for was beyond this religious
environment. I remember being in church and having
some confusion with guilty feelings. I often left feeling full
of fear instead of filled with God's presence. Through *my*
lens, Jesus loved and accepted all beings as Divine. The
Jesus I knew expressed love and compassion for all
humanity no matter what color, race, belief or choice a
person made. My whole life I've felt a strong connection to
Jesus and I still do. Through this relationship, I express
my love and gratitude for his Divine presence.

I trusted my inner guidance to lead me to what I
was searching for although I had no clue what I would
find. In the fall of 2003, I took a trip to the Northeast and
experienced a powerful weekend that gave me some
insight toward what I was seeking. I will never forget that
weekend in Richmond, Virginia. It was November, late
autumn, and the leaves were falling from the trees. There
was still a vast array of reds and yellows but anyone who
is familiar with this season knows the foliage has passed
and winter is settling in. I was delighted to be there. The
coolness in the air was a treat and it felt really good. I was
there to meet my cousin for the weekend and to celebrate

1

our birthdays. I turned 37 that year and I was single. She and I were excited about any time we had to spend together because we lived far apart yet we were close, like sisters. I was in the midst of trying to find myself and asked my cousin if she wanted to join me at this workshop. She wasn't as excited as I was. In fact, I had to talk her into it.

She had every reason to be hesitant because this wasn't your ordinary workshop. I flew from Florida to Virginia just to attend. My cousin drove from Philadelphia. We decided it would be good to do some inner exploration together. I thought it would be good for me to learn more about myself. Little did I know at the time I had a lot to learn. I had been divorced a few years but never dealt with any of my emotions around splitting up with my ex-husband. It was like I stuffed them down inside my body. Worse than that, I was in total denial that I had lost custody of my son. As time went by, I realized there were many other circumstances that I hadn't worked through or dealt with. It seemed that it was the right time in my life to be taking a look at situations that caused me to become numb. It was the right time for me to do some inner healing.

Rebecca and I met late afternoon on a Friday. I wasn't at the hotel; I was next door at the local drinking establishment. When she arrived, I was feeling the effects of the alcohol and perhaps a bit overzealous to see her. She was disappointed that I was already drunk after recently dealing with her own mom's struggle with alcoholism. I cleaned up my act as best I could and we started the workshop. The next day was a full day and the expanded hotel conference room was packed with at least a hundred people. As the participants laid down their blankets and pillows, the facilitators spread out across the room. Half the group did their breathing session in the morning and in the afternoon we would switch.

### An Altered State of Consciousness

When it was my turn to breathe, I got right into it. I was lying on my back and started the deep continuous breathing. The idea was to let go into a deep process, an altered state of consciousness or a deep meditation. It was not an easy process because with so many people in the room and the loud music, it felt difficult to let go. I wasn't sure what to expect but I stayed with it.

The first thing I experienced was an inner vision of rainbow-like colors. The colors were mostly blue and purple. It was fascinating to experience these cloud-like colors in my mind. Then something suddenly shifted and I felt like I was some place underground. It felt damp. It was dark and cold as if I was deep beneath the earth. I have to admit, I was a little scared but I stayed with it because I was curious. The next thing I sensed was a box near me. Someone spoke to me from the tomb-like box. The voice felt feminine to me. She whispered, "Open the box." I thought, "What, no way, I don't think so." She said, "Don't be afraid." I thought to myself, "Easy for you to say." This dialogue in my head encouraged me to open the box. Finally I said, "Well, why not?" This is all an illusion anyway, no harm done. I opened the box. As I did, this huge purple presence seeped out of the opening and enveloped me. I was instantly relaxed and felt calm and supported. This feminine presence lifted me up. We swirled up and out of the darkness to be revealed in the light. We were above ground and floating in the air. I said, "Who are you?" I felt this presence was familiar to me and I wanted to know if this was true. I heard the voice say, "Aynanya." I asked again, "Who?" The syllables I heard spelled....ay-nan-ya. I thought, "Wow! That's interesting; I will have to remember that." As the experience continued, she and I danced together in the sky, we were free and joyous. There was nothing holding us back.

When this energetic presence emerged from the box, like a puffy, purple hue, I felt as though I was participating in an awakening. It was as if this energy had been dormant for thousands of years and I helped lift the veil. This feeling was an amazing correlation of lifting the veil and breaking free. The session went on for almost three hours. There were other experiences intertwined but I mostly remember the details of the connection with this feminine presence. Yet, I had no idea who she was.

3

After the breathing sessions were over, we all drew a picture to continue the experiential process through creative expression. I drew an opening from a box that had a purple hue around it and a dancer-like pose emerging from this opening. I drew the eyes that I saw in my mind and I tried to represent the paradoxical image I felt of light and darkness entwined. I'm not much of an artist, but drawing the artwork was helpful for me to process more of it. I even wrote her name, Aynanya, at the bottom of my artistic expression.

The day went by fast, it was evening already and time to share highlights of our session with the rest of the group. The group energy was different than the night before because everyone had undergone this deep meditative process. When it came my turn to share, I was not sure how to explain what happened. I did the best I could but it was really beyond me. I looked at my drawing in front of me and mentioned the name I heard in my head. My cousin noticed something peculiar when I was talking; the woman across the circle had a name badge that was spelled almost the same as Aynanya. After the sharing, we went up to her. She said she was given that name from her teacher and that it was based on an ancient language comparable to Sanskrit.

The experience that day was so powerful that it eventually transformed my life. It was no longer about that experience, it evolved into a much deeper meaning. Although the experience was beyond words, I somehow found the language to express it. After I went home, I wrote in a journal the details of what I experienced:

> In the darkness, I felt entrapped. The walls were closing in and there was no where to go. Just then, there was the slight possibility of opening the sarcophagus. I tried and it opened. I was enveloped by an extraordinary presence. I emerged from this dark space and immediately was embraced by the color purple. I felt this hue of purple surrounding me like a large, supporting cloud. I felt like I could touch the purple, it

4

was palpable. Then, the ascension, we were light as a feather, as if we had wings. We rose up to the light and we were dancing, like free floating ice-skating, in the sky. I was in complete and utter joy. Every cell in my body felt free, dancing elegantly. My heart spilled wide open and my energy felt expansive. I was floating and I was free and I was with this beautiful Divine presence that I did not even know. I asked her name, she answered, "Aynanya."

It was necessary for me to keep writing about the experience. That was my only method of integrating this experience and I was grateful I had that to work with.

## A Slow Process

This experience of a feminine presence was bewildering and always on my mind. Yet it was a slow process for me to find out more about her. Honestly, I had no idea that I would find anything more about her. I wrote many poems about her but I never knew who or what I was referring to. The experience stayed with me for a very long time and it continued to nag at me. Months went by before something would trigger or recall my memory. I tried to identify with Hindu or Buddhist deities and search the right words to find something on the internet.

Finally, I got a break. I met a woman who was a Native American wise woman. I told her about my experience and the name. She had some insight to whom I was referring to. She printed some material for me to look up. This information spelled the name as Inanna. The flood gates opened! I found all kinds of information about a Goddess Inanna from five thousand years ago simply by changing the spelling. I was delighted and intrigued. Right away I ordered two books that focused on Inanna's story and myth.

Several months went by before I was able to fully grasp the content of these books. But when I did read them, one at a time, I was in awe. The story line and the symbolism correlated to my own life and I had uncountable "aha" moments. I completely resonated with the development and experiences in these books. Now, eight years later, I am *very* familiar with the story of this ancient goddess. Sometimes when I am meditating, I feel her invoking well-being and resilience in every cell of my being. I have learned so much about myself and about her through this deep connection with her legend that I found myself writing a whole book about her.

### The Unfolding

I opened up to the unknown when I took that trip to Richmond because I was looking for something more. I went there with no idea what would surface. My soul searching led me to a deep connection with a feminine presence. At the time of the workshop, I apparently wasn't ready to deal with my personal issues. Instead I experienced a Goddess emerging from my psyche. How was that supposed to be helpful? Before too long, I was able to find some answers to that question. I allowed the process to slowly unfold—like an onion, peeling away one layer at a time—and the answers appeared when I was ready to understand.

I have spent the last three years writing my own interpretation and identification of Inanna's story. I hope you find her story just as fascinating as I do. This Goddess landed in my psyche as a mystery. I sat in wonder, anxious to open the box. What I discovered inside was better than the outside package. What I discovered changed my life! Now, I want to share this gift with you. At a minimum, I hope you get a taste of my passion for revealing this beautiful Goddess from ancient Mesopotamia. She exists as a presence within me the same way Jesus lives within my heart. Overall, my intention is for you to discover a whole new perspective of feminine energy that will perhaps unveil **your** inner Goddess.

# Chapter One –
# Ancient Myth &
# The Feminine Archetype

*It takes a lot of courage to release the familiar and
seemingly secure, to embrace the new. But there is no real
security in what is no longer meaningful. There is more security in
the adventurous and exciting, for in movement there is life, and in
change there is power. ~Alan Cohen*

For thousands of years, stories have provided paradigms for the process of healing. Although we have discovered written stories dating back to the 3rd Millennia BC, the origination of storytelling in the oral tradition is unknown. Many of these stories have been translated from an ancient language to English and are understood either literally or symbolically. Over time, the discovery of myth and the archetypal realms have become a therapeutic tool for searching outside of oneself to experience what is happening within (Jung, 1961). The foundation of this book is to share the story of an ancient Goddess from 5,000 years ago. Much like any ancient story, it contains rich symbolism that can be used as a tool for self-growth. Utilizing symbolism and myth, I give examples of my own life that provide a back drop for healing based on an archetypal, objective perspective.

The story of this ancient Goddess is very powerful. It was found written on clay tablets in the 1920's. The archaeological dig was in a location we now call Baghdad. Although some important pieces were missing, over time the matching tablets surfaced from other international museums. To date, the most complete translations of this story have been published and are easily read as historical literary prose that is more popular for college coursework than it is for self-growth. Yet, this powerful, erotic and riveting story has far more meaning to us through an archetypal identification because it contains the basic elements of myth that resonate with our internal process. This journey of the Goddess Inanna includes strength, courage, love and wisdom comparable to any other historical myth. What makes it special and concurrent with modern times is the basis of the story—it's about the life development and empowerment of a woman who lived thousands of years ago.

### Myth and Life Development

Myths are intended to help people identify with the experience of life. They often include rich symbolism translated from scholars to help us identify and resonate with pivotal moments. In human life, it is common for people to feel that they are on a quest or a search for meaning. Joseph Campbell, the author of *The Hero with a Thousand Faces*, tells us:

> Myths are the stories of our search through the ages for truth, for meaning, for significance. We all need to tell our story and to understand our story. We all need...help in our passages from birth to life and then to death. We need life to signify, to touch the eternal, to understand the mysterious, to find out who we are. (1949)

Campbell strongly believed that myths are the clues to our spiritual potential in human life. The Goddess Inanna's myth reveals the elements to our spiritual potential through storytelling and symbolism. To help you get a bigger picture of what the Goddess Inanna represents, I will give you a brief summary in this chapter. Before I do that, I want to give you a little background on how her story became public knowledge.

### Kramer's Translations

Inanna's story was translated by Sumerian scholars starting in the 1940's. They translated these cuneiform writings over a thirty to forty year span of time. It is very important to take into consideration what was happening in those times that would have skewed the scholars' perspective. For instance, women in this country were not considered to hold a high office. Women were expected to be homemakers and yield to their husbands or fathers demand. The scholars had this in mind when they were translating the myth of this ancient Goddess. According to their translations, she was evidently on the top list of deities representing supremacy over the Sumerian pantheon. The cuneiform translation shows Inanna is Queen of Heaven and Earth and also noted as Goddess of Love and War. Therefore, we have not just one but two very interesting titles that were given to Inanna by modern archaeological scholars.

Samuel Noah Kramer is most likely responsible for noting her prominent status as he had dedicated most of life's work to the Sumerian culture and to Inanna. In fact, the main crucible for his book was to acknowledge, *Inanna: Queen of Heaven and Earth* (Wolkstein & Kramer, 1983). Kramer died a short while after co-authoring that book but he left us with an autobiography. He shared intimate details of the struggles he faced in compromising with his fellow scholars. His colleagues were not in agreement with his translations because scholars are subject to societal beliefs of their time. But if we can let go our beliefs and open up to the astounding creative mind, we can expand our awareness for the mystery of evolution. Kramer was able to do this. He trusted his beliefs and his own truth. He understood that times change, people change and views change. If we were to find these cuneiform tablets a couple hundred years earlier they might very well have been destroyed. If we were to find them now, in the 21st century, they may have a different translation or interpret a more modern perspective.

Although Kramer's perception of Inanna as a powerful deity was evident through all of his translations, he too was subject to the beliefs and knowledge of his time. In my own experience of working with these literary translations, my viewpoint varies slightly from what Kramer published in 1983. Based on my educational

9

credentials of energy (thru Traditional Chinese Medicine) and my background in Transpersonal Psychology, I see a story of a powerful woman that represents an important message about a woman's life development. From an objective standpoint, I incorporate the chakra energy to accentuate this development. This is my central theme. I envision Inanna's myth as a template from which to map a woman's life while aligning the similarities through the psychospiritual aspects of the chakras.

As a feminine archetype, Inanna represents a courageous woman and a spiritual warrior. This archetypal woman is not subject to control and she is neither meek nor whimsical in her stance. She is fearless. For this reason, I think the early scholars were intimidated by her myth and not so apt to put her on a pedestal.

Kramer, however, was not intimidated at all. In fact, based on his autobiography, he had a personal relationship with Inanna (1986). I can relate to Kramer's connection because I, too, have a relationship with Inanna that was based on my encounter with her presence. This relationship grew over time. Kramer suggests this happened with him as well. In his autobiography, he attributes this relationship to his success. He says, "Who was responsible for starting my ascent, the rise in my Sumerological fortune? No one other than the bright, white Goddess Inanna!" Kramer adds that Inanna became his guardian angel and this relationship continued to develop throughout his whole career. He makes a powerful statement regarding the modern woman:

> Inanna is the one Goddess...whose deeds
> and powers should serve as a soothing
> balm to the wounds of liberated women the
> world over. Brave, crafty, ambitious,
> aggressive, awesome, but also desirable,
> loveable, and passionate, she was glorified
> and extolled throughout Sumer's existence
> in myth, epic, and hymn. No one, neither
> God nor man, dared oppose her, stand in

her way, say her nay. And neither can I.
(Kramer, 1986)

His relationship with her was driven by his passion to give her the rightful status she deserved. Kramer is no longer here to give us all the details of his experience but I am so grateful for his autobiography and his lifelong research on the Sumerian culture.

What happened five thousand years ago is written in stone, but none of us speak or write that language anymore. The closest we can come to understanding this translation is through scholarly interpretations. However, we can find some relatedness to this story and do research to back up a theory. This is what I have done throughout this book. For the last nine years I have studied Inanna's myth and developed my own interpretation about her story. My hope is that more people can relate to her story and benefit from my translation. Further, that it can help assist in the transformation our world is experiencing today.

Our human race is going through a spiritual crisis whereby many people are struggling and discontent. On the opposite spectrum, others are on a fast paced spiritual quest. This book will look at chaos vs. quest and integrate the two operating as a whole. This concept is based on the yin/yang philosophy of nature. In order to evolve, we must begin to recognize that all parts of life are an aspect of the whole.

### Balancing Light and Dark

This concept of yin/yang or "darkness within the light" is not new. Vaughan-Lee, a modern day Sufi mystic, recently wrote a book titled, *Alchemy of Light: Working with the Primal Energies of Life* (2007). Vaughan-Lee says "We live in a culture that respects little apart from surface glamour, the trappings of worldly power and material possessions." In order for us to survive and evolve we must shift our way of thinking. One way to approach this concept is simply accepting that darkness is a part of light. Light and darkness can be integrated and balanced.

Once we accept all the parts of our inner Self, we awaken to the truth.

In Vaughan-Lee's book he summons us to take responsibility and continuously cultivate our own inner light. This will not be easy, he says, and it will require letting go of greed and the power hungry ego. Also, we will be required to let go of a surface image based on materiality and success. This will be the most difficult aspect for our society to let go of. However, Vaughan-Lee has a vision. He knows that we are capable of taking responsibility and being in service to humankind. He says, "With each individual moving toward the light and accepting responsibility, change will come—change that overturns our unconscious and destructive nature" (2007). A new era will emerge that shifts our way of thinking. Vaughan-Lee says, "There is a good chance this change will involve emphasis on the archetypal world." He encourages us to cultivate a relationship with the archetypes as a doorway for transformation in our individual consciousness. Through acceptance and respect we can form alliances with the archetypes.

Vaughan-Lee explains that archetypes are alive within each of us yet we have lost touch with them. However, if we are willing to make a conscious connection with these existential forces, Vaughan-Lee says, "we can overcome being sucked into their raw power." Otherwise, they will remain lurking deep within our shadows. I was lucky to experience a connection with a powerful feminine archetype in a Holotropic Breathwork™ session (see Appendix A). I now have a relationship with this archetype which allows me to understand the deep paradoxical dynamics of my inner being.

Inanna's title, the Goddess of Love and War, is a significant and powerful indication of paradox. Inanna was an important deity to the ancient Sumerian civilization. The Sumerians understood the world of opposition based on universal laws. They lived in a lush, pristine paradise and they honored the paradox of nature. Light and dark, yin and yang, interior and exterior, good and evil, masculine and feminine—they honored all aspects of wholeness.

Sadly, our western society does not recognize these properties inherent in our everyday lives. It is not so much that we ignore this reality of opposing forces in nature as much as we are not aware of the concept in our thinking. Because of this we have missed the bigger picture. In several Sumerian hymns honoring Inanna (see Chapter 7 and 8), the emphasis of honoring all contradictions of nature is obvious. These hymns were being sung to recognize the intrinsic wholeness that exists in the universe.

One of the most important pieces to begin recognizing both light and dark aspects of our nature is to face our own shadow. The darkness within is the hardest to see. We can better understand and change our perspective by taking a look within through an inner lens that accepts the darkness within the light. This is a central theme worth exploring for all human beings. In fact, Vaughan-Lee says, "by accepting the truth of our inner worlds we will be free of fear and the anxieties that grip us." This is the only way to embrace the light. Once we accept all the parts of our inner Self, we awaken to the truth. Through this awakening, we find compassion for others and accept our family, our friends and loved ones inner worlds. We can accept them as human beings doing the best they can no matter what their issues or patterns may be.

### Discovery of Archetype and Myth

Through identifying with ancient myths that recognize nature as a symbol of dark and light, death and rebirth, we can relate to a new evolutionary truth. Carl Jung, the famous Swiss psychologist, implemented myth and archetype as a therapeutic tool for psychotherapy and self-growth. Jung describes using archetypes as a way of searching outside of oneself to experience what is happening within. Through the development of archetype, Jung implemented the concept of shadow.

According to Jung, the "shadow aspect" is part of the unconscious mind consisting of repressed instincts, weaknesses and shortcomings. "Everyone carries a shadow" Jung wrote, "and the less it is embodied in the individual's conscious life, the blacker and denser it is" (1932). For example, the shadow of someone who believes they are kind may unconsciously be harsh or unkind. There are many examples to list. The shadow represents everything that the conscious person does not wish to acknowledge within themselves. More importantly, Jung emphasized the importance of being aware of our shadow aspects and to incorporate it into conscious awareness in order to avoid projecting it on others.

Although I have not studied any formal Jungian Psychology, I am familiar with its benefits. In this book, I will share with you how I have used myth and archetype to see outside of myself to experience what is happening within. Below I have given you an overall summary of Inanna's myth. Additionally, I will share areas in my life where I have awakened to my shadow self. Through identifying with a Goddess, I became aware of areas in my psyche that were keeping me blocked from future growth and development.

### Her Story in a Nutshell

The Goddess Inanna was a prominent deity, well-known five thousand years ago, in the location we now call Baghdad. We meet her as a young woman who courageously faces the forceful flood waters of the Euphrates River. She graciously plucks the lone cedar tree that risks being torn away in the storm. She brings the tree to her holy garden to nurture and care for the tree. She tends to the tree and imagines how big the tree will become as she looks forward to making a throne and royal bed from its trunk.

Inanna discovers her feminine virtue as she lies under an apple tree pondering a visit to her father, the God of Wisdom. Her hopes of attaining the principles of civilization are ripe. Enki, the God of Wisdom, is very happy to have Inanna as a guest in his home and they celebrate by drinking beer together. In his drunken state, he decides to give Inanna all of the powers of civilization. Inanna is thrilled until Enki wakes up, looks around and says to his servant "where are the powers of civilization?" His servant replies, "You just gave the powers of civilization to Inanna." Enki regrets doing this and sends his servant to retrieve and return these powers. However, Inanna is a very courageous woman. She stands up to Enki's servant. She is confident; she does not flinch in her mission of bringing the powers of civilization back to her city of Erech.

In the next stage of her life, Inanna's story focuses on her courtship and sacred marriage ritual with Dumuzi. Inanna is the decision-maker of who will become the best partner and King of Erech. She must choose between the farmer and the shepherd, but the shepherd is more assertive, so Inanna chooses him. They have a wonderful courtship and a big, festive marriage celebration. More importantly, Inanna and Dumuzi have a passionate and sensuous consummation. The lyrical quality of their love is very similar to the Song of Songs in the Bible.

Not long after Inanna and Dumuzi are married, he becomes preoccupied with his kingdom. Inanna is a bit dismayed. She hears an inner call to visit her sister in the underworld, "From the Great Above, Inanna opens her ear to the Great Below." Most people would not heed to this call because it is common knowledge that journeying to the underworld is like going to your own funeral. No one returns from the underworld alive. However, Inanna is a fearless woman. Her trip to the Great Below is filled with rich symbolic detail that centers around seven gates. At each gate, Inanna must remove a particle of clothing until she is left naked and vulnerable. Before Inanna is free from her journey, she must find someone to replace her. Who does Inanna choose? Unless you already know the answer this will remain a mystery until a later chapter.

### A Spiritual Quest

Journeying to the underworld or any journey is symbolic of a search for finding one's own truth and inner purpose. Stanislav Grof, M.D. and Licensed Psychologist, describes a "spiritual quest" as having an experience that is vitally important and a crucial aspect of human life (2010). The symbolism of Inanna's journey to the underworld indicates the importance of these experiences in life and represents stages one must conquer. This underworld experience of her journey is perceived as a natural cycle of life or an evolutionary death and rebirth.

According to ancient and modern mystics, every human being is capable of letting go, surrendering, or experiencing what is called a "dark night of the soul." This is considered to be a spiritual rebirth or an awakening. When a person goes through this process of transformation they suddenly become more connected to the spiritual realms and recognize the importance of being in service to humanity. Jesus experienced a spiritual rebirth after dying on the cross and being entombed for three days. The Buddha experienced a spiritual awakening when he left the palace to be a witness to human suffering. All of the ancient and modern mystics have experienced some form of transformation that is retold and shared with others to help realize that this is a normal application of one's life experience.

I underwent my own turning point or "dark night of the soul" a few years ago. My husband and I experienced a deep loss. His son took his own life. This tragedy was so devastating that I went inward and experienced a very dark, introspective time. This experience was not comfortable, but I survived. I didn't physically die. Instead, I gained a new perspective about life. I learned to trust in my intuition and guidance. I now feel a sense of inner freedom that I didn't have before and my conscious thoughts feel more clear and awake.

Symbols like "journeying to the underworld" are congruent to our modern times which indicate we must continue the trajectory to develop our inner spiritual energy and cultivate Divine presence in everyday life. We must return again, on a daily basis, to remember who we are—spiritual beings living a human life.

### Chakras

One way to connect with spiritual energy is to identify with the chakras. The chakra energy can be viewed as a

16

psychospiritual approach to a healthy trajectory of human life. Inanna's stages of life match this development.

The seven chakras of the human body hold secrets of personal development. Inanna's story assists us in identifying with this energy. It is an invisible, unseen energy that exists within every human being. We can utilize it to live our life purpose and to reach our highest potential. Our growth and expansion are dependent on our awareness and ability to make conscious choices. If we have no recognition or knowledge of this energy, we may form unconscious reactions that keep us trapped in difficult patterns.

The lower chakras have to do with our own creation story, our sense of belonging and to the physical aspects of life. The heart chakra is all about compassion, for oneself and for others—it connects the lower and upper chakras. The higher chakras have to do with our progression and later stages. The later stages in life allow us more time to develop our spiritual sense and to be in service.

The word chakra is a Sanskrit word, which means "wheel" or "disc." Chakras are located in the center of the body from the base of the spine to the top of the head. There are seven chakras spinning in the body's energetic system, each a circular wheel of light associated with certain colors, elements and function. By learning to tune into this energy, we can begin to embrace the fullness of who we are.

If we can integrate the psychospiritual aspects of the chakras in our daily lives, this will benefit our overall health. The awakening of Kundalini works much the same way because it focuses on the chakra centers. Inanna's story aligns with the upward progression of the chakras and the upward movement of energy in Kundalini Yoga.

What is Kundalini?

Kundalini simply means serpent or snake in Hindu and is represented as feminine in nature. It is the vital energy that lies dormant at the base of the spine until it is called into action. There are various means through which it can be activated. The most common is through practicing Kundalini Yoga. I will explore the concept of Kundalini in more detail in the second chapter because it relates to the root chakra—this is where the Kundalini or serpent energy rises. To further understand Kundalini Yoga and the chakra energy system, read Appendix B. The nature of Kundalini allows us to clear old, stagnant cycles and empower us with a trajectory that leads to a "Kundalini awakening" or a rise to our full potential.

### The Feminine Archetype

As a feminine aspect of cosmic and human powers, Inanna is dual in character and manifests the full gamut of human potential. In one sense she is Mother Earth, her concern and caring for others is marked by her rescue and tender care of the *hulluppu*-tree. She manifests Gods gifts for mankind and stands strong and confident in an effort to do this. In another sense, she represents the capacity in every human being to triumph over difficult times and continually achieve fuller expressions of Divine glory.

In today's world, women do not necessarily have a strong female archetype to identify with. Women are being called to unite and bring light to this feminine Goddess energy. As the modern woman awakens, she will find it helpful to identify with a legendary story that signifies women's confidence, strength and feminine virtue. This is not a matter of feminine power vs. masculine power; this is a matter of taking responsibility for our human development.

Women have a great capacity to take on major change but we must prepare and empower ourselves to do this. The same way Inanna hears an inner call, women are being called to get in touch with their feminine principles and take responsibility. This will manifest as a healthy balance of masculine/feminine equality. Now more than ever it is vital that women bond and come together to implement a universal shift in consciousness.

Inanna's story has been fascinating for me. As I surrender to a path of self-discovery, I feel like I am given clues and direction. I have many examples in the chapters ahead that will utilize and portray my life story viewed through the symbolism of this feminine archetype. Each segment will contain themes that most women can relate to. The following is one example of how Inanna's story helped me. It serves as a template for understanding how archetype and myth can help someone heal or develop further through taking an outside approach to a personal matter.

## A Personal Transformation

Just a few years ago I experienced an internal crisis. One of the ways I got through this crisis was identifying with Inanna and her sister. Inanna's sister, the Goddess of the Underworld, is known to be quite wicked and mean. Inanna is curious and decides to visit her sister in the underworld. Before she meets Ereshkigal, she is asked to remove all of her clothing. Inanna meets Ereshkigal naked and bowed low. Ereshkigal "fastens the eye of death" on Inanna without question or hesitation (see Chapter 6).

When I relate this story to my life, it is not a literal interpretation rather an archetypal identification. By relating to an archetype—the same way characters in dreams are used to understand a situation—I experienced an outward reflection of what was happening within.

Based on the scene of Inanna and Ereshkigal meeting, I could relate to a confrontation with a nemesis. When I lost custody of my son, my ex-husband's girlfriend controlled the communication between me and him. Over and over, I had to deal with her telling me what the visiting schedule would be. This felt like torture and with each passing day, I felt like I was being stripped of any control regarding my son, Clinton. I couldn't believe I was dealing with some woman telling me how and when to raise my child. The emotions I felt over losing primary custody of him were difficult enough but then I had to contend with her. There were several instances where I lost my cool and let her know what I thought but she always found some way to manipulate the situation. She liked to "dangle the carrot" over my head and often threatened to not let me see Clint. After too many years of that, someone was bound to die. I was already mortified so I surrendered to my ego with the realization that it was far more important to have a relationship and spend precious moments with my son than to argue with her.

I changed my perspective based on Inanna and Ereshkigal representing the light and darkness of the whole person. I took a look at my own dark aspects; I began to own my shadow. The crucible of this action was instigated by my son telling me, "Mom, you are just like her." I could have easily denied that statement (and I initially did) but children can be great teachers if we listen closely. When I did that, I had a change of heart. I realized that we don't ever know what activates people to do things. Some people experience anguish from deep-rooted childhood issues. Maybe my son's "stepmom" was hurting inside and acting out of fear. I had a glimpse that she really was a good person and just didn't know how to show it because she was protecting herself. It took a lot of strength for me to hold her in the light, especially when I was dealing with such a sensitive situation. My son and I love each other. I knew that if I saw her through a different perspective, one that made her and I both spiritual beings of light, I felt better and more at peace.

Through this process, I learned so much more about myself. I was given the opportunity to take a look within through a lens as if I was her. Identifying with this ancient myth was helpful because I began to see my situation from a different perspective. By doing this, I instantly felt compassion for her inner turmoil. In Chapter Six, I will share the details of this episode between Inanna and Ereshkigal and explain why people react emotionally to protect their own deep suffering.

### Experience the Wonder

In the chapters ahead, I invite you to expand your mind and emerge into a space of consciousness from five thousand years ago. This story is inclusive of a civilized society that was just beginning. In ancient times, people used symbols to communicate. These symbols still relate to us today and can be portrayed as clues or a map for our life development.

Each chapter in this book has its own unique feel to it—each representing an upward progression of energy in the body. Keep in mind, Chapter Two is especially dynamic because it introduces the rhythm of each chapter. It begins to compare Inanna's story with the chakras and integrates my life examples relating to that theme. This chapter also develops framework relating to the three centers of the body the same way Inanna grows, nurtures and develops her *hulluppu*-tree. Chapter Three is brief but offers a comprehensive understanding of Inanna's feminine nature and incorporates the ability to create and experience intimacy.

Chapter Four will explore our goal-oriented, egoic self. This can manifest as good or bad, depending on your perspective and outlook on life. Chapter Five is by far the loveliest chapter because it integrates the heart space of our bodies, showing the importance of love and compassion for others. Chapter Six relates Inanna's "journey to the underworld" with a modern day "dark night of the soul." Chapter Seven and Eight hold a high status, one few of us attain in early life. It is expressed with respect, stature and reverence.

Inanna's story is a gift for humankind. In her story, we can embrace all the aspects of our feminine nature into one magnificent and powerful Goddess. Is her story a myth? Myth has a deeper conjecture of make believe whereby stories are more factual. The answer really depends on the artifacts of history, the belief system of a culture and how well we identify with a story. Jesus' life story is taken as a literal translation for many people, as well as the story of Siddhartha transforming into Buddha.

The most important thing to take away from these stories is that we can identify through the symbolic, figurative personification of these characters. They are equally good examples of living a life devoted to a higher Self. Moreover, these stories tell us the importance of honoring a "spiritual quest" and believing in one's personal truth.

When relating to Jesus' life, many people have heard or used the common acronym WWJD (What Would Jesus Do)? We can ask the same question about Inanna. What would Inanna do in certain stages of life development? The answer to that question lies in the following pages of this book. The symbols in this book are hopefully some you come across in your life. If and when you see them, I hope you remember, reconnect and enjoy the "aha" moments of synchronicity and Divine intervention. Lastly, I hope you enjoy this interpretation of Inanna's story—it is through a modern woman's lens.

The next seven chapters are based on human development and our spiritual nature. Inanna's story will be segmented based on the design and interpretation of the clay tablets from which it was originally found. Each chapter begins with a temple poem translated by Samuel Noah Kramer. He spent many years translating these poems. In *Inanna: Queen of Heaven and Earth,* he collaborated with Diane Wolkstein to offer a woman's perspective (1983). In this book, *Unveiling the Modern Goddess,* the poems have been slightly moderated from their original version. My intention for including the poems is to give the reader the basis of Inanna's story and highlight the spiritual nature of an ancient language. If the reader is interested in knowing the complete version written by Wolkstein & Kramer, it was published in 1983 by Harper & Row: New York.

The Sumerian poems are followed by my interpretation of symbolism based on modern day living. Each chapter describes and compares the psycho-spiritual aspects of the chakras with Inanna's development. The purpose of interweaving the myth, symbols and a pertaining chakra gives the reader a modern day perspective to relate too. Moreover, through the gift of ancient storytelling, we can identify with myth and archetype to reach our highest potential and to better comprehend what it means to unveil the modern goddess!

# Chapter Two –
## Beginning With the Tree

*Great tree of bliss! Your swaying braziers*
*Musk each second with Eternity!*
*I wade incessantly in your sea of star-flowers*
*Your trunk soars blazing from my heart.*
~Rumi

*In the first days, in distant primeval days,*
*In the first nights, in far-off primeval nights,*
*In ancient days when everything vital had been nurtured,*
*In ancient days when everything needed had been provided,*
*When bread had been baked in the homes of the land,*
*When earth had separated from heaven,*
*When heaven had been moved away from the earth,*
*And the name of man was fixed;*

*In those days, a lone tree, the hulluppu-tree*
*Was planted by the banks of the Euphrates River.*
*The South Wind arose and pulled at the lone tree's roots.*

*A woman, Inanna, plucked the tree from the river.*
*She brought the tree to her holy garden,*
*She settled the earth around the tree with her foot,*
*She wondered, how long until I have a shining throne.*

*Then a serpent who could not be charmed*
*Made its nest in the roots of the tree,*
*The eagle-lion bird set his young in the branches*
*And the dark maid Lilith built her home in the trunk.*

*Inanna wept, yet the creatures would not leave her tree.*
*She called her brother asking for help*
*And Gilgamesh, the valiant hero, stood by Inanna.*

*Gilgamesh lifted his bronze axe and entered Inanna's holy*
*garden.*
*He struck the serpent who could not be charmed,*
*The Anzu-bird flew with his young to the mountains,*
*And Lilith ran into the wild, uninhabited forest.*

*Inanna and Gilgamesh exchange gifts.*

*From the trunk of the tree,*
*Gilgamesh prepares the royal throne and bed for his sister,*
*She hands him the pukku and mikku*
*Inanna, in turn, hands Gilgamesh the keys to the kingdom.*


This is the beginning of Inanna's story. In this epic Mesopotamian tale, Inanna is introduced with a fresh start after the floodwaters rage through the lands. She steps in like Mother Nature. She represents nurturance and protection for all of life. Inanna saves the lone cedar tree in an attempt to establish a relationship with humankind. Every culture has its own story of when life began. Every one of these stories makes you want to believe that it is *the* beginning. Inanna's myth is one of the first stories ever written, or at least one of the earliest that we know of (Campbell, 1949). It could very well have been transformed through the retelling in many different traditions and cultures.

Along with the beginning, every culture has a creation story. In the ancient Sumerian culture, the creation story begins with the Gods separating earth from heaven. The Gods created human beings "to be in their likeness" and to serve the Gods (Kramer, 1972). In the Hebrew Bible or Old Testament, the book of Genesis tells us man was fashioned from clay to rule the animals. In the Babylonian version, man was created to serve the gods and free them from the need of working for their bread. According to a Sumerian poem, which antedates Hebrew & Babylonian literature by more than a millennium, man was fashioned of clay to free the gods from laboring for their sustenance (1972). This poem combines both the Babylonian version and the Hebrew version. Thus, the oldest known intention of the gods was to create humans to serve the gods and provide for their sustenance.

Many of us have heard the story of our own "beginning." Parents love to tell their children about their birth. Stories help us link events throughout our lifespan. Our birth story could very well be the most important one we know. According to Stan Grof, a leading transpersonal psychologist, it's imprinted on our soul (1985). From an

24

esoteric perspective, there are a myriad of beginnings and endings that span our whole life. As we ponder the symbolism of our own life cycle, let us take a look at a very ancient story that provides a backdrop for human life and the earliest formation of civilization that we know of today.

### *The Beginning of Her Story*

The beginning of Inanna's story is about a young woman who is willing to brave the forceful flood waters in order to save the tree of life. This tree, called the *hulluppu*-tree, represents life. It is about to be pulled from its roots by the force of the South wind. The South represents the future and the powerful onset of change. According to Jane Goodall, the symbolism of the South represents the power to love (1984). As the tree dangles, barely alive and clinging for life, Inanna rescues the tree. Inanna loves the tree and she willingly cares for the tree while watching it grow and flourish. She brings it to her "holy garden" with every intention of looking after it and protecting it just as a mother looks after her young.

This tree represents a foundation from which to grow and form. From dangling roots, it is nestled in Inanna's holy garden and blessed with a fresh start—safe and protected, supported and loved. This tree represents the creation and development of human beings. The symbolism of the tree of life is a cosmic tree, rooted in the waters of the underworld, and passing through earth to heaven (Fillmore, 2005). The tree of life has a wide range of meaning but overall it represents human growth. Inanna recognized the tree by its very form as a metaphor for evolution—its trunk represents "unity" and its branches represent "diversity." The tree of life can be viewed as the inherent life of an organism; symbolized in the physical by the nerves and the spinal column. The spinal column represents the tree. The nerves which carry the living waters are the branches that produce leaves and fruit on the tree (2005).

In Sumeria, the tree of life was the cedar tree. Cedar is a symbol of power and immortality (Tresidder, 2000) Thus, life must be properly nourished and cared for before it can take root, grow and flourish. This tree becomes a metaphor for the whole of creation. It grows on a sacred mountain or paradise and a fountain of spiritual nourishment will gush from its roots. The tree of life and the flood waters are well-known symbolic metaphors. In this story, the raging flood waters wipe out and cleanse all life forms on earth. Water represents the physical, emotional and spiritual cleansing and the power of renewal.

The tree of life is our upward development and our ascension from the root chakra to the crown of the head, producing fruit and spiritual illumination. Inanna is in favor of saving humanity because she understands that human development requires guidance and a spiritual connection. She also knows that beginnings take time and require patience, nurturing and care. Inanna is willing to devote herself to the tree with the intention of manifesting spiritual illumination. She creates a visible blessing of Divine nature when she brings the tree to her holy garden. The holy garden symbolizes earth and a paradise of the cosmic order (Herder, 1993). Inanna knows that we are all a part of the cosmic order which is represented by our consciousness and the spirit within.

### Developing A Strong Foundation

After Inanna brings the tree to her holy garden, she waits. She patiently watches the tree grow strong and form a solid trunk. Inanna knows the importance of growing a tree that is well rooted to earth. The trunk is its foundation. As the trunk grows, Inanna yearns for a throne and a royal bed. Both of these material features are symbols of her purpose in life. From the throne, Inanna will have a solid base from which to manifest her role as Queen. From the royal bed, Inanna develops her feminine virtues. Inanna is excited about these manifestations and is willing to be patient.

The beginning stages of any creation are first to imagine what we want. Without imagining and visualizing we leave ourselves open to the universe creating and manifesting for us. Many years go by while Inanna waits for her royal throne and bed. In that time, she is very attached to her tree. One part of human nature is that we want—we all crave and yearn for something. When we are in this human body, our journey involves manifesting what we wish for. Inanna wants a foundation by which to rest and to create. The royal bed and throne are formed from wood. Wood is a solid matter and a significant element representing earth. The tree grows strong from a rooted, solid trunk which has to break ground and grow upward. Any foundation or manifestation of this nature takes time.

### What Manifests in the Tree?

Inanna's *hulluppu*-tree grew and was quite solid. When Inanna was ready to transform her solid base, she was surprised to find creatures inhabiting her tree. The three creatures are the snake, the "wild" Lilith, and the *anzu*-bird. They become impersonal representations that manifest from a single seed.

According to Carl Jung, we all begin as a seed. "Within this seed we have two aspects, two paths available, the personal and impersonal. If we choose we can hang out in the roots, entangled and entrenched in the muck. Or, we can germinate and move upward with the impersonal Kundalini energy as it takes us to a higher perspective; one in which we experience a full realization of the Self" (1996). For Inanna this full realization is the three creatures that inhabit her tree. Inanna chooses to utilize the impersonal path. Based on the universal symbolism of these creatures, each one represents a very rich and interesting interpretation. Overall, the snake, the "wild" Lilith and the *anzu*-bird signify the three centers of the body—namely, the lower center, the heart center and the head.

### The Coiled Serpent

Snakes are related to the root chakra, the very lowest part of the human torso. This chakra is often related to an upward spiraling serpent—specifically in Kundalini Yoga.

This type of yoga uses the image of a serpent to travel up the spine or chakras thus "lifting up" or activating the spirituality and radiance of life. The symbolism of the snake or the snake's duality is a balance between fear and reverence (Tresidder, 2000). Throughout ancient history, snakes are identified in various ways. In some cultures,

the snake is the oroborus and symbolizes rebirth. In other cultures, the snake is considered evil or bad luck. This salvation or release from a cycle of being begins in the roots and the snake is there coiled and waiting for action.

If we think of the tree as a metaphor for our human body, then it all begins by nurturing and caring for the body. The roots of the tree leading to the stump represent the lower center of our body. This is our solid foundation and base. In Inanna's story, she plucks the tree of life in order for humanity to ascend from its lower nature toward spiritual illumination. This is the beginning. We must connect with our body before we can connect with the mind or consciousness and the awareness of our spiritual Self.

*A Fresh Look at Lilith*

The wild Lilith is content in the trunk of the tree. She makes her home in the center of the trunk. If we relate to Lilith inhabiting the center of the tree then she clearly represents the heart center of the body. This center of the body represents our human connection to feel love and compassion for others. According to historical data, Lilith represents our uncontrollable, primal instincts including desire and narcissistic behavior. She is often represented as the dark, power hungry maiden. Although Lilith doesn't seem very compassionate, keep in mind that her story has been interpreted and is subject to one's egoic perspective. Lilith goes far back in history and has toted a bad name from early on.

In the book of Genesis, Lilith is Adam's first wife. She would not lie beneath him because she wanted equality and respect. Lilith runs off to the wild, uninhabited places because she refuses to be controlled and demeaned. Eve comes along and is portrayed as the wife who surrenders to Adam and submissively lies beneath him. Yet she is blamed for desiring the fruit! Symbolically, the apple represents fertility, bliss, prosperity and desire. Fruit is good for us, we should desire it.

From a metaphysical point of view, when we eat the fruit of the "tree of life" we appropriate ideas of Divine life (Fillmore, 1931). Through this Divine love and through awareness we learn to be compassionate, loving human beings. This capacity is embedded in every one of us. If we stay conscious of our motives and intentions, we get closer to God. When we try to tame our wild inner Self, suppressing our fear or grief, we no longer enjoy the fruits of life. Instead, we live in a prison of fear and denial and survive through a shadowed lens.

By resisting our "wild Lilith"—our primal, feminine nature—we form attachments to things that have no benefit for our long-term growth and survival. This prison eventually encapsulates our physical body and our mind and causes us to disconnect with the primal forces of nature. In contrast, by relating to this primal nature we awaken to universal truth. The truth is everyone is subject to emotions that make us react unconsciously. Awakening to conscious awareness expands our capacity to love instead of restricting it.

When we know and embrace this "wild Lilith" within we can make choices to stay present and choose to see the Divine in another's eyes. We are able to see the truth and the truth sets us free. We are consciously able to change everyday patterns that would otherwise keep us trapped. We are reborn in a new awareness that enlightens all of our actions and allows us to be civilized.

Moving upward, the *anzu*-bird places his young in the crown of the tree. The *anzu*-bird has a lion's body with eagle wings. This manifestation in the crown of Inanna's *hulluppu*-tree represents the head center of the body. The lion represents courage, initiative and fearlessness (Fillmore, 2005). Every human has the capacity to enter fearlessly into life and the ability to understand all things. Yet, depending on our upbringing and the beliefs we are exposed to, we convince ourselves that this is not true. If we simply changed our thought process, we would see that all things are possible. Courage is necessary but courage alone is not enough. Due diligence and persistence are key ingredients too. Most important, we must have a devotional attitude and a connection to spirit in order to receive spiritual inspiration.

The eagle-lion bird represents spiritual growth and holding a vision. By realizing the connection of the higher Self, or the spiritual Self, one has the capacity to be free. We are given a direct clue to focus on inner wisdom. We lose the ability of connecting with a higher knowledge if this part of our body is closed off. We will not be able to spread our wings, to believe in our Self and reach our highest potential. This is the bird of paradise—the place where we can be completely free. Connecting to the heavenly realms gives us a glimpse of the afterlife.

This head center or crown of the human body is a key ingredient to our perception of immortality. Very few people are able to reach this stage of development which allows the crown chakra to stay open. These few, however, are known throughout the world and live from all three centers of the body; the trunk, the heart and the head. They live with the knowledge that we come from the same source and in essence, we are all one.

Humanity has existed through ten thousand years of evolutionary growth. My hope is that this current transformation will take us to the next level of our being, a place where we connect with the energetic aspects of our three centers, and a place where we can utilize the knowledge in these parts of our body to survive and inevitably transform.

### Striking the Bronze Axe

Inanna asks for help when she finds the creatures inhabiting her tree. Her earthly brother, Gilgamesh, comes to the rescue. Gilgamesh represents the yang or masculine energy of the self. He strikes the serpent with his bronze axe which is necessary to activate the upward energetic action of the internal chakra energy. In Kundalini Yoga, there is a strike or mode of activation that starts the waves of movement up through the chakras and the spine. Striking the metal indicates activating structure and order. Gilgamesh represents the logical, reasonable principles of human life. Inanna knows that masculine strength oriented towards action is necessary for civilization.

Contact with the tree brings Sumerian man and woman to a deeper understanding of life's elemental forces. Furthermore, this contact allows for a balance between male and female conveying respect on both parts. Equality in leadership is paramount to a growing, thriving civilization instilling trust and respect for each other. With this vision, the people of Sumer prosper.

Inanna's dream of having a throne and royal bed comes to fruition. In gratitude, Inanna hands Gilgamesh the "keys to the kingdom" by presenting him with the *pukku* and *mikku*. The *pukku* and *mikku* are translated as the staff and/or rod and reel. These gifts are made from the branches of the *hulluppu*-tree and represent power and immortality. Gilgamesh represents solid matter, substance and strength and Inanna represents the eternal effervescent energy of life. When we are ready to open our minds and hearts to the truth will we see that the infinite and eternal are right there in our hands.

In the *Epic of Gilgamesh*, the story begins with Gilgamesh getting the "keys to the kingdom." But he drops them and they fall into an unreachable crack in the earth. Gilgamesh is the great King of his city. He spends his whole life in search of these keys—even sends Enkidu, the wild man, to help him find them (Kramer, 1971). The legacy of Gilgamesh can be perceived as a symbolic attempt of our own reach for some inanimate object outside of ourselves.

The keys will continue to remain in mother earth until we recognize that she is our connection to immortality. Now is the time to go inward and recognize the gifts of our Divine Mother. The heavenly paradise is ours to see only if we have the faith to believe that it is so. The source, the connection to power and immortality, lies within.

Our human, innate nature strives for balance and harmony. By bringing balance to opposing forces, instilling equal attention to both the masculine and feminine in all areas of life, we have a better chance of surrendering to the Divine. That balance existed in a time when our ancestors worshipped an all-knowing, all-embracing Goddess named Inanna. We experience this balance when Inanna and Gilgamesh share their gifts. By recognizing both masculine and feminine orders of nature, we can move forward into a new paradigm. It is very likely this new world order will create a civilization unlike any other generations or ages before us (Campbell, 1986).

Humanity in general is still operating from a masculine viewpoint. The majority of people in a civilized country view their life based on the outside material world instead of the inner self. However, it is time to look within, to connect with our inner feminine energy. We can do this by immersing in Mother Nature and asking for help. This help may require some healing on our part. One way of healing and connecting with the inner feminine energy is based on the energy of the seven chakras. The root chakra is the most important because we must first connect to earth and develop a strong, supportive base before the energy can flow upward into the other seven chakras.

### The Root Chakra

The root chakra is located at the very lowest center of our torso. Its red energetic wheel circulates and forms energy downward like a three-legged stool. This feels like a solid, stable base and an energetic connection to Mother Earth. Like a tree with a solid trunk, we are rooted to earth. We begin to relate with our physical bodies through the root chakra. If we are taken care of, we feel safe and secure. As we grow, we are given the opportunity to develop a strong, solid foundation that helps keep our root chakra healthy. In the book, *The 7 Healing Chakras,* Davies says, "The root chakras main function is to keep us grounded in the physical world and it keeps us alive" (2000). The root chakra grounds us to earth.

The root chakra is all about form and matter. This relates to our human physical needs and our attachments which translate to a fear of loss. Through the root chakra we get a sense of physicality. In a physical world, we are subject to material things and the need for substance, shelter, clothing and other comforts to appease our physical needs. The root chakra also governs our basic instincts. We have primal instincts like eating, sleeping, sex, self-preservation and survival. If we have a good relationship with our primary caretaker we will likely develop a good foundation. The importance of nurturing the root chakra is vital to security and self-esteem.

If we have a strong root chakra we feel safe and have the underlying sense of belonging to a family, group or significant other. We feel we can trust people. We feel we have everything we need. In this current age, it is common to take simple needs for granted. Think back to ancient times when there was no running water. Many cities were built near water because it is necessary for human survival. Dry seasons were detrimental and often caused tribes to move. They were aware of their basic needs being met because they were essential to their nourishment as human beings. It was considered blessings from the Gods and Goddesses to have everything they needed.

In the modern world, having a roof over our head and having food, could mean having everything we need. Yet having a TV and a refrigerator also translates to satisfying our basic needs. The list could continue when we are living a luxurious lifestyle; then our needs become more material and we cannot think of living without them.

It is okay we have evolved to this, we are human beings and we desire material things. However, we also have desires beyond our basic needs.

We desire love or we yearn to be in a relationship. We inherently desire to be motivated mentally through intuition, intellect or a universal Divine wisdom. We crave a connection to others and we desire mental and spiritual nourishment. These desires are motivated by the heart and head center in Inanna's tree of life. The root chakra is the area in our body responsible for personal survival, security and a strong connection with Mother Earth. When we have a solid base, this fuels our growth and development.

In its healthiest form, the root chakra springs forth like a fountain of energy. The root chakra can be the most important chakra as it governs the development of our entire life. Unfortunately, not everyone has a functioning or healthy root chakra.

Some people did not get their basic needs met in early life development. If we don't get our basic needs met as a child, we can be subject to feelings of vulnerability and the human psyche begins to produce an underlying sense of fear. This fear can show up in many different ways depending on the situation.

Some examples of a dysfunctional root chakra can manifest as dissociating, questioning the value of life and disconnecting with the physical body. One can feel as if they don't belong. Without a strong root chakra and a lack of awareness, one can feel like a tree without roots that can be easily swept off by a flowing current. The good news is that the limitations caused by a dysfunctional root chakra can be overcome.

### Kundalini Yoga & Carl Jung

Kundalini Yoga is a dynamic, powerful tool for healing and expanding awareness in one's life. When practicing Kundalini Yoga, the cycle of energy starts from the root chakra and flows upward through the body. The root chakra is activated via some force that begins a trajectory up into the higher chakras to create balance and harmony. This upward motion through the chakras falls outward, like a fountain, and is brought back down to the lower center to be released. Yogi Bhajan, a famous guru of Kundalini Yoga says, "By creating the prana (life energy) in the cavity and mixing it with *apana* (cleansing energy) and taking it down and again bringing it up. This is Kundalini" (Khalsa, 1996).

Carl Jung discusses the root chakra and Kundalini Yoga in a seminar given back in 1932. He suggests the root chakra is merely a seed and it is in the bottom of the trunk that things begin. "In the great body of the cosmic world the trunk holds the lowest place, the place of the beginning." As our conscious grows and evolves from our trunks and becomes an embryo, "it is slowly seen as a full-grown tree." He affirms that the world of consciousness is only a seed in the future and that through Kundalini Yoga pulling the embryo upward will activate one's Divine nature. This order rises in levels represented through the chakras. Jung calls them new worlds of consciousness or a natural development—each one above the other. With each level, we experience and learn very crucial lessons. This is how Inanna's story unfolds. With each segment of her story, development ensues and she passes the test. In Jung's lecture, he tells us:

> It is exceedingly important that you are rational, that you believe in the definiteness of the world...the world is made of a culmination of history...otherwise you remain detached from the [root chakra]-- you never get there, you are never born. There are plenty of people who are not yet born because...they have not formed a connection with this world; they are suspended in the air; they are neurotic (1932).

It is important that we are born into this world because the purpose of this world is to realize the self. Jung passionately and clearly states that "we must make our mark in the world, form roots and do the best we can to believe in the most absurd things." The shoot must come out of the ground, which is the *linga* sparked by a personal mark. Inanna's initial mark is rescuing the tree of life. This is followed by manifesting creatures that inhabit a tree.

According to Jung, most people do not emerge from the roots of their being. They stay entrenched. He says, "We are entangled in the roots, and we ourselves are the roots. We make roots, we cause roots to be, we are rooted in the soil and there is no getting away for us because we must be there as long as we live" (1996). Many people stay focused in the lower center of the body; the first, second and third chakra. They never find what it takes to emerge from the greed, lust and power that rules their lives. They stay rooted and grounded in the energy of the material world. On the other hand, living in the ethereal realms without any sense of being "grounded" isn't ideal either.

In my life development, I recognized that early on I did not nourish the healthy aspects of my root chakra. I had a hard time connecting with this energy and instead lived in the illusive, spiritual realms. Living in the energy of the upper chakras was not wrong, I just did not benefit from its full potential. In earlier years of my adult life, I was not grounded enough to influence people in the way I had hoped. My stability and sense of trust were unhealthy and I literally acted as if I had no substance.

### Washed Away?

When I look back to growing up, I was indeed supported by my family and felt safe and well cared for but something was missing. I remember feeling a need to belong and I was always searching for it. I struggled to ever find it. On more than one occasion, I felt like that dangling tree on the Euphrates River. I lacked a strong connection to earth. My connection to nature always felt good but my spirit seemed to defy a gravitational pull.

I have very little memory of my childhood but some specific things really stand out. When I was 13, I made my first attempt of suicide. Life, to me, was becoming increasingly complicated and difficult. I found myself deeply depressed and unhappy. It felt like there was a force against me and I was struggling to be present in the world. My hormones were kicking in and that meant I had to be in my body. Yet my tree of life was on thin ice and there was no brave Goddess to come down and rescue me.

I was not sure why I had these rollercoaster emotions all the time. One day I would be in a deep rut and the next day I was overflowing with the joys of life. I didn't have any basis or psychological foundation from which to draw. I was completely alone in my head and I couldn't control it. The emotions would take over me and there was no way out. I remember feeling lost and confused and wanting out. There was a discord with what was going on in my body.

I remember the scene, it was early evening. I was in the bathroom and I could hear my family talking in the living room. They were going on about their normal business. I remember they were laughing while I felt like my world was caving in. I couldn't take it anymore, or so I thought, and wanted out. I took the razor blade out of my shaver and started to slit my wrists. It hurt and it wasn't easy. I didn't bleed very much because the razor was dull but I managed to create noticeable markings. After a long period of time, I opened the door and swiftly ran to my bedroom to crawl under the covers. I believe this is all I really wanted—some sort of escape.

### Round Two

In my second year of college, I was 18 years old. Even though I seemed like I was taking care of myself, I often felt disoriented. Some people perceive drinking in college as a normal part of this experience but it can be seriously damaging for some young students. It can create imbalance and disharmony in one's psyche.

This is what happened to me when I had been out drinking one evening. My thoughts of suicide were heightened because I was drunk. When I got home, I felt very alone. I did not feel like I fit in. In my desolation, I decided to swallow a handful of pills and then began crying incessantly. I began feeling sorry for myself while I envisioned my funeral and who I would miss. Not long after, my roommate came home. She and I had been best friends from our hometown and we were roommates since our first year of college. Jeni knew something was awry because she heard me sobbing. I told her I took the pills and she immediately rushed me to the hospital. I was in a daze. The only thing I remember is being in the emergency room and drinking something that made me vomit.

After that incident I didn't talk to anyone. I went about my regular routine the next day. I didn't talk to my friends or family about what happened. My friends kept an eye on me but they never addressed me directly even though I had some idea they knew.

Those are the only two times I remember attempting suicide in my youth. However, I remember feeling as if I didn't belong here all of my life. When I was in this space, I honestly felt there was no hope and all I experienced was darkness. All in all, I felt as if I was going through a continuous cycle of death and rebirth. I didn't want anyone to know and I would continue to smile as if nothing was wrong. When I got past those dark, gloomy days I would be happy and full of life. This mental exasperation would continue to haunt me into adulthood and it became dangerous territory in mid-life (explained in Chapter Six).

When I had my son, I finally felt a sense of purpose. I knew I could never leave him. This was the first time I felt a stable connection to earth but I continued to have thoughts that I didn't belong. Recently, in the last couple years, I realized how important it is to have a practice of grounding my body. The key for me is to stay aware of this. If I knew this when I was younger, I may have had a different experience.

*Sprouting my Shoot*

On a positive note, I had a lot of drive and determination when I was young. My mom called me, "Miss Independent." However, it could have been fear driven when I made the decision to get a college degree. I was aware of some of my friends demeaned and beaten by their boyfriends and I was fearful of becoming helpless and controlled by men too. I decided to build a strong foundation and base for my future. The serpent energy was there in my root chakra, waiting for me to activate it, but I didn't know how to manifest this for a healthy outcome. What manifested was my "wild Lilith" nature crying out for validation.

If a woman ignores or is unaware of her inner Lilith nature, she will be controlled by it. One very common example to explain this concept is when a woman is in her menstrual cycle. If she is unaware of her emotional mood swings, she may show up like a bitch or like she is untamed and out of control. In the popular book, *Women Who Run With Wolves,* the author, Clarissa Pinkola-Estes, speaks of how important it is to own the wild woman within (1992). In addition, she says it is equally important to search for a mate that will honor this aspect.

Earth is a great metaphor to recognize the importance of honoring and expressing our primal nature. Our beautiful Mother Earth wants to be acknowledged and recognized for her wild, untamed nature too. Environmental activists are constantly trying to protect our land and water. In the meantime, we get full expressions of Mother Earth's uncontrolled emotions; whether it is a ravishing sunrise or a catastrophic event.

### The Feminine Emergence

Women are taking a stand and reclaiming their historical virtues because it is our primal nature. This intrinsic nature is instinctual survival. We all want to continue our human race and survive. This is a part of who we are. It may be automatic or unconscious, but the sooner we recognize it, the better off we will be. Women have a great capacity to connect with nature and to a Divine source. Those with a deep inner knowing are capable of surrendering to higher wisdom. The eagle-lion bird manifesting in the *hulluppu*-tree represents our human capacity to make conscious choices and to utilize self-knowledge.

From an "eagle eye" perspective of Inanna's story, she is a young woman who braves the forceful flood waters of the Euphrates River and saves the "tree of life." Our own modern day "tree of life" is hanging by a thread. Many people are beginning to recognize this based on the current uprisings in the Middle East and the recent natural catastrophes—namely Japan. What if we had some way of preventing this from occurring? What would this look like? This could look like the beginning of Inanna's story when she brings the ragged cedar tree to her holy garden. As a recourse, this signifies a need to start connecting with humanities inner feminine nature.

When I mention the feminine, I am not referring only to women—I am referring to both men and women. Women and men both contain feminine and masculine energy. These two energies exist simultaneously within each human being. However, very few of us utilize our inner feminine *nurturing* nature.

Inanna represents a woman who contains a balance of masculine and feminine aspects. She is strong and empowered. She takes action. Moreover, Inanna's myth tells us she is willing to rescue the tree and has patience to nurture the tree. In our modern world, we need to move forward and acknowledge the Divine feminine. We must recognize this Divinity within ourselves. Very much like Mother Teresa is revered for her feminine qualities of nurturing and caring, women too should be valued for their innate skills of loving and leading their families.

Women are beginning to recognize their inner feminine qualities and there is a recent trend of women valuing the importance of self-care. Mothers who care for their families are coming of age to realize that it is okay to take some time for themselves. The influx of women taking yoga classes or yoga teacher training has significantly increased. True yoga allows one to go inward and meditate on the inner feminine energies. The next step for women's evolution is to honor their own inner truth.

Women will begin to lead the way in their family's health and in their family's set of values. If a woman is healthy in mind, body and spirit, she boasts a healthy

40

family. If a woman is unhealthy, however, the family is subject to shadow aspects that easily trickle from generation to generation. If the family household is of mind, body and spirit, the children pick up on this and it sets the stage for their perceived values. A man who criticizes his wife in front of his children leads his family to believe this is normal and continues creating turmoil. On the other hand, a man who is raised by an empowered female will naturally generate a balanced family.

Clearly, Inanna leads the way for her city of Erech. She is not afraid to stand up for what she believes in. Throughout the next chapters, you will find many instances where Inanna honors the importance of her feminine equality. This is a great example for the modern woman to follow in her footsteps.

The only way women will make a difference in the trajectory of our human race is to stand up for what they know is true in their hearts. Furthermore, they can reunite with their primal, innate instincts. Women can honor the magnificence of their feminine cycles and embrace the continuous change in their bodies. Women should not be ashamed of their menstrual cycle or try to stop it through birth control injections. This is their womanhood. Feminine virtues should be perceived as a gift; a blessing for the creation of human life. This insight will help us stay better connected with the whole of our human nature.

To summarize, the lower center identifies with our physical needs or desires, our range of emotions and our commitment or purpose in life. The heart center reveals layers and levels of compassion ranging from loving another to loving all sentient beings. Someone with a very open heart center lives without attachment and judgment and has developed a practice to establish a relationship with a Divine source. The head center is where we connect with the internal wisdom and higher Self.

Inanna often listens to her inner wisdom, she does not ignore this inner voice—she quickly responds to it no matter what the consequence. She follows her inner guidance to lead the way not only for her own purpose in life but for that of her city.

In Chapter Three, Inanna is on a mission to visit her Father, the God of Wisdom. They honor each other's masculine and feminine qualities. They do this by drinking out of the vessels of *Urash (Mother Earth)* and by eating butter cake. This was the favored offering to the Gods & Goddesses. In some scholarly interpretations, Inanna seduces the God of Wisdom and she is responsible for intentionally getting him drunk. This is viewed by some as her cunning and malicious intention to steal the powers of civilization. Let's look at a different perspective for the relationship of Inanna and the God of Wisdom, one that predates the Bible and perhaps has more of an altruistic viewpoint.

# Chapter Three –
## Desire & the Apple Tree

*Everything flows out and in;*
*Everything has its tides; all things rise and fall;*
*the pendulum-swing manifests in everything;*
*the measure of the swing to the right*
*is the measure of the swing to the left.*
*~The Kybalion*

Inanna placed the crown, the shugurra, on her head.
She went to the sheepfold, to the open land.
She leaned back against the apple tree.
When she leaned against the apple tree,
Her vulva was wondrous to behold.
Rejoicing at her wondrous vulva,
Inanna, the young woman, applauded herself.

She said:
"I, the Queen of Heaven, shall visit the God of Wisdom.
I shall go to the Abzu, the sacred place in Eridu.
I shall honor Enki, the God of Wisdom, in Eridu.
I shall utter a prayer to Enki at the deep sweet waters."

Inanna set out by herself.
When she was within a short distance of the Abzu,
He whose ears are wide open,
He who knows the me, the universal laws of heaven and earth,
He who knows the heart of gods,
Enki, the God of Wisdom, who knows all things,
Called to his servant, Isimud:
          "Come, my sukkal,
          The young woman is about to enter the holy shrine.
          When Inanna enters, give her butter cake to eat.
          Pour cold water to refresh her heart.
          Offer her beer before the statue of the lion.
          Treat her like an equal.
          Greet Inanna at the holy table, the table of heaven."

Isimud did as Enki requested.
Then Inanna and Enki drank beer together.
They drank more beer together.
They drank more and more beer together.

*With their bronze vessels filled to overflowing,*
*With the vessels of Urash, Mother of the Earth,*
*They toasted each other; they challenged each other.*

Inanna is quite satisfied with herself as she places the crown of the steppe—the prairie—on her head. She even applauds her wondrous vulva in the "sheepfolds" under the apple tree. She is not ashamed of her sexuality or her desire—she knows that pleasure is a human gift. Her femininity and desires are what make her who she is. Sitting under the apple tree, with the crown on her head, Inanna contemplates and creates. In Sumerian, the word for crown is *shugurra*. This represents the beginning of her womanhood marking an important rite of passage. The apple, in ancient symbolism, represents fertility. Greek, Celtic and Nordic mythology all describe it as the miraculously sustaining fruit of the Gods, thus signifying immortality. The apple also represents sexual or non-sexual bliss and is linked with the vulva shape of the core in long-section. It is a common emblem of love, youth and springtime (Tresidder, 2000).

### Inanna's Journey to Erech

The next step in human development is cultivating a relationship and communing with others. Flaunting her raw feminine vitality, Inanna's journey begins with her feminine eminence and she rejoices. Sensible, wise and seductive Inanna plans to visit her father, the God of Wisdom, for help. Her father Enki gladly welcomes Inanna's presence and calls forth her feminine qualities. Enki's servant prepares the butter cake and beer to celebrate Inanna's visit. They both look forward to their meeting.

Inanna and Enki celebrate by drinking beer in their overflowing bronze vessels. Inanna is excited about her plans and shares this with her father. She can confide in him and share her creative desires. She is able to freely express herself and tell her father what she wants and what she plans to create.

Her father supports her and although they are not intimate in the way we think of intimacy in modern day, they are very private and personal with each other. This relationship between father and daughter or between masculine and feminine is not only very important for the growth of a woman's life, but it allows for balance in all of humanity. A mother and son relationship is equally important. If we experience an imbalance of this natural relationship it can create a future discord with intimate relationships. It can also inhibit our creative flow.

Inanna has the flow of energy within her that wants to create. Inanna knows her father will honor her and support her desire. After all, they are in agreement about the growth and fruition of civilization. Diane Wolkstein, folklorist and co-author of *Inanna: Queen of Heaven and Earth*, suggests that in today's world, women still use their sexual wiles to get what they want. She says, "Using beauty and sexual prowess, women succeed" (1983). Similarly it is natural for men to be easily charmed by a young woman who carries a bit of innocence or "purity." Sometimes this charm results in the man "giving away his power."

Father Enki is the God of Wisdom and Water. Water can be understood simply as the flow of life. In nearly all of the ancient cosmologies, we can associate water with purity, fertility and the source of life (Tresidder, 2000). In the Bible, water represents the sea and is represented as our mental potentiality of the conscious (above) and unconscious (below) (Mark 6:47-51). Thus, we have the term, "the sea of consciousness."

### Inanna and Enki Celebrate

Inanna and Enki celebrate each other and symbolically acknowledge their venture in producing prosperity. They celebrate with joy and camaraderie and are able to fully embrace each others desires. They eat some delicious treats and drink beer. Beer in ancients times represents the "presence of a well of water, the depths of life and truth in [human] consciousness, which will spring into everlasting life when he makes proper contact with it"

(Fillmore, 2005). Here we again find the element of flowing water, only now it is shared between masculine and feminine energy. These two deities understand desire and the overflowing abundance of life, finding deep pleasure in physical senses and emotional balance.

Inanna and Enki are drinking "the flow of life" out of bronze vessels. They drink out of the "vessels of Urash, Mother of the Earth." Holy vessels are a symbol of comprehending our ability to appreciate life, love and truth (Fillmore, 2005). This cup or chalice can be a vessel to provide nourishment and overflowing abundance. The chalice may be widely connected to the Holy Grail symbolizing the drinking of spiritual illumination or knowledge, liberation and hence immortality but it is also a symbol of women's fertility and the womb, thus signifying a container for human life.

In our modern times, fertility seems only to be related to sexuality and producing a family. Fertility, in ancient times, reaches far beyond these two aspects by including the reproduction of fruit or the harvest in nature. It is about prosperity and abundance in life. Hence, the cup overflows through our desire and pleasure in all aspects of the earthly realms. Without desire, we do not know how to identify with our passion or pleasure principle.

We are sexual, emotional human beings and we were created to have feelings and desires. This emotion is a gift from the sacral chakra. It is here we find joy in the material realms. These ideas become more significant as we mature and recognize that intimacy is more than sexuality. As we develop our awareness of this concept, we make choices to seek those desires.

Desire is manifested by a constant flowing energy; it keeps us in a forward, constant motion. It moves us in this trajectory of truth toward our purpose in life. Fear only blocks this energy. Fears are old thoughts or unmet desires that keep us stuck or blocked (i.e., the shadow). With fortitude and grace we can release these constrictions and allow our inner light to shine. The Divine light within is activated by desire and propels our chakra energy upward.

Through a connection with others, we nurture our need for touch and sharing our feelings. One way we can share our joy or that of our loved ones is through celebration. Inanna honors the joy of the human race. She brings joy that is playful and free-flowing. She sparks imagination in children and gives us the desire to dance, to enjoy feasts and festivals, to celebrate and have fun.

In any type of partner relationship, we are bonded through intimacy. We are sensual beings. It makes sense to seek touch with other beings and to explore our sexuality. But we also want to feel love and compassion from those that are closest to us. Cultivating a healthy intimate relationship with others first requires us to be intimate with ourselves. If we initially develop strength and security, rooted and growing like a tree, then we grow into adulthood with more willingness to be open to others.

### The Sacral Chakra

The sacral chakra's sense is taste. The element is water and its function is simply to keep everything flowing. This flow pumps the solar plexus into action. That is why a healthy sacral chakra, focused on desire, allows access to periods of accelerated empowerment or learning. In *Anatomy of the Spirit,* Carolyn Myss said we have greater potential than we ever believed possible—this chakra primes the pump to enable us to achieve it (1996).

We are human beings and we desire material and physical things. We desire food and drink. The sacral chakra is to blame if we take our desires too far. If we act out in gluttonous behaviors, we can damage our lives and the lives of those around us. Individuals are subject to addictions and other mental illnesses such as depression or compulsive-obsessive behavior.

Drinking and celebrating go hand-in-hand for some people. When Inanna and Enki drink beer together, they think nothing of drinking too much because they are celebrating and having a good time. I grew up in a family that liked to celebrate and enjoy "spirits" with each other. It seemed natural from my perspective as a young adult. I thought everybody celebrated like my family. It didn't occur to me that some people do not drink alcohol. Later, I learned that some people do not even celebrate or show any intimacy within the family dynamics.

### What is Intimacy?

Our childhood, even up to our early adult experiences, can paint the picture of how we perceive this joyful, sacral energy. I remember as a child having a close relationship with my Mom and Dad. Every night I had a routine of kissing them goodnight and saying "I love you" before running off to bed. Looking back on this as an adult, I realized I was the only child in the family who did this. This display of affection came naturally to me.

As I grew into my teenage years, I was still very close to my parents. But one day the closeness my Dad and I shared was lost when we he criticized my creativity. I started writing poems when I was twelve or thirteen. I had written a poem about life being difficult and not worth living. This poem ended on a positive note. It was titled *Life is Worth Living*. I showed my Dad and he laughed—he ridiculed my writing. He totally discounted the poem by telling me I don't know anything about the trials and tribulations of life. His last response was devastating. He said, "What do you know, you are just a kid." I opened up to my father, I trusted and confided in him and what I got in return was sarcasm and mockery. This struck deep. What I thought was my best poem was scoffed by my father. I was devastated and it would be years before I showed anyone else my poems.

Father Enki validates Inanna's creativity. This part of Inanna's story is significant because it emphasizes the importance of a father honoring his daughter in order for her to develop self-esteem. My creative, sacral energy froze up because I was criticized.

When it was time for me to date, I was given stern instructions that the only way I could go on a date was if the boy picked me up and came into the house to meet my Dad. The only issue with that was no one ever asked me out. Perhaps this had to do with my blocked creative flow which affected my sacral chakra energy. I never had an opportunity to develop a healthy, intimate relationship with the opposite sex when I was a teenager. Instead, I flirted with older men to get attention which led to unhealthy circumstances and dreadful memories.

On one occasion, I was at an outdoor party where everyone was drinking and smoking marijuana. An older man, that I thought was my friend, asked me if I wanted to smoke a joint. I said, "Sure," and followed him to his car. He said, "Get in, I'll turn the heat on." It was winter in Chicago. Before I knew it, he had me locked in, pinned down and he raped me. I went into shock and was unable to speak to anyone for the rest of the party. I sat alone on the outside of the fire circle and cried. No one addressed me and no one asked me what was wrong. I was unable to speak. The next day my friend said she heard a rumor I had sex with this guy. I denied it because I blamed myself and realized how stupid I was for trusting him and going with him to his car.

Another memory I have as a teenager is when I flirted with an older guy while I was working at a deli shop. He asked me if I wanted to go for a ride on his motorcycle. I thought it was cool that he wanted to hang out with me. I enjoyed having someone pay attention to me and wanted to believe that this man really liked me. As an adult, I realized how unhealthy this circumstance was and that this guy was strange. Worse yet, he was over twenty-one and I was only fifteen. I did not know this was considered an illegal relationship in the eyes of the law.

At that point, I had unconsciously lost my sense of self-respect. This only added to my lack of stability and support in my earlier adolescence. At such a critical time in my development, I was unable to grasp self-confidence and build my self-esteem. Unfortunately, these ill-actions created a skewed perspective that affected my future growth. Luckily, I have had a chance to reflect and heal some of these past situations that have negatively influenced my life.

From a developmental perspective, I was desperate to experience intimacy, to belong to someone or to have someone like me. I was searching for an outside validation but what I really needed was to find it within. Through self-growth and inner work, I realized how these experiences affected my perspective regarding intimacy. I thought sex was the only way to experience intimacy. Now I recognize that true intimacy comes from a deep, personal place that extends beyond a physical act. When we are able to experience the joy of another's passion, or the joy of another's dream, we can celebrate this joy and experience intimacy.

This is the true meaning of Inanna and Enki's celebration—they are sharing their joy of creative pleasure and delighting in that moment. Let's consider these two characters in a modern day representation. The daughter is on her own, she is independent and taking care of herself and she calls her Dad and says, "Hi Dad, I am coming home for a visit!" He is super excited and goes all out to celebrate her visit. The story isn't too far off what would take place in modern times. A woman who is supported by her father has a better chance of cultivating healthier relationships overall.

When a father celebrates or outwardly approves of his daughter, she has a much better chance of feeling confident and empowered. Perhaps this is the reason why the father walks the bride up the aisle in our modern day wedding ceremony. The detail of this ritual has been vacant and seems to have lost its emphasis in our western society. It would be much more powerful for women if it was considered a "right of passage" into womanhood. By the father approving the daughter's union with another, he celebrates and validates her.

### Reclaiming Self-Confidence

Fortunately, my father and I had a chance to rectify our relationship in a very symbolic way. On the first day of the millennia, January 1, 2000, I had an opportunity to spend the day with him. I had been spending a significant amount of time with my parents over the holidays and my Dad and I were bonding in a refreshing new way. I stopped by to wish them both a "Happy New Year!" but my Dad and I ended up sitting outside by the pool all day and having a great conversation. The scene and setting were perfect. We lounged in front of the crystal-clear water of the pool and celebrated. I remember my Dad saying "this is as good as it gets" and repeating that phrase over and over again along with how much he loved my Mom. He shared with me how blessed he was to have her in his life and that she has taken good care of him. It was so sweet to be witness to his intimate feelings and that he was open to sharing them with me.

He and I talked about my dreams and aspirations. I wanted to go on a month long sabbatical and work on my poetry in Bali, Indonesia. He said "Just do it Karen, just do it!!" He was encouraging me to follow my dreams. This was very different than the reaction I got at thirteen. My Dad's approval of this trip was especially exciting for me because I had anticipated a negative response. Running off to Bali, and traveling alone to a foreign land, wasn't exactly an everyday thing to do. I was asking for his approval and he gave me a loud and resounding, "Yes!" I wasn't aware at the time it would be the last thing he said to me.

It wasn't until much later I realized the importance of this celebration and that we had once again bonded and connected on an intimate level. I will never, ever forget that day with my Dad—it was the last time I ever saw him. The next day I got a call from my sister. She said Dad had a heart attack and died. I went into shock and started crying uncontrollably. I didn't stop crying that day—my tears flowed creating a river of grief for my Dad.

I loved my Dad very much. He was a very influential person in my life. I did eventually stop crying and was able to sing a song for him at his funeral mass. I wrote the song when I was a teenager. I regretted never having the courage to sing it to him personally, but fortunately I had given it to him as a poem on his 65th birthday, just six months before he died.

> For you Dad,
> I've written this poem,
> To thank you for loving me
> And giving me a happy home.

For you Dad,
I'll sing you this song
To make you feel so good
For always being strong

For you Dad,
I will hug you so tight
And hope it makes up for
The times when we would fight

For you Dad,
I will say I love you
And know that it is true
Because no one else could have
A better Dad than you...

### My Journey to a Foreign Land

The last thing my Dad and I talked about was my trip to
Bali, Indonesia and attending a month long writer's
workshop called: *The Way of the Artist.* Four months after
he died, I followed through. There I was, all alone, in a
foreign country. I was thousands of miles from home when
the floodgates opened up and I began crying again for my
Dad.

The natives on the island of Bali were having a big,
festive cultural event in Ubud—the cultural center and
main city in Bali. We were two week's into the writer's
workshop, hosted by Naropa University, and everyone
except me, went to the festival. I wasn't feeling well so I
decided to stay back at the bungalow and rest. I had
stomach cramps from swallowing a drop of water. The
cramps were so bad I thought I was going to die when
something came over me. My Dad was gone. I would never
see him again. The cork opened and out spilled all my
grief and guts. Hours went by while I poured my heart out
for the loss of my Dad. I was glad no one was around to
witness my pain because I was able to fully express
myself.

I was able to really grieve and feel the loss. For
many years, I had blocked myself from feeling anything.

After experiencing that catatonic release, I felt more integrated and grounded. Every now and then I still shed a tear for my Dad, but mostly I remember how happy he was. His words, "This is as good as it gets!" goes through my mind from time to time. Now when I hear someone say it, I smile and think of him. I'm so glad he was peaceful and living his life in the moment. It doesn't get any better than that!

Returning home from Bali was a big relief because I missed everyone and I was worried about my Mom. But one of the pitfalls of the sacral chakra is being susceptible to human addictions. It wasn't long before I was drinking again. I thought for sure my trip to Bali would cure me of me of this, but it didn't. However, because of Holotropic Breathwork™, I was a bit more aware and in control this time. This work made a huge difference in my transformation by allowing me to express my inner emotions. I slowly but surely began to heal and re-connect with my sacral chakra energy.

### Holotropic Breathwork Helps Addictions

One very powerful way to be free of bad habits and stay awake to addictive behavior is to do Holotropic Breathwork™. This technique, developed by Stan and Christina Grof, allows one to take a look at what is going on inside their psyche. According to Grof, people can connect to their inner healer and experience varying feelings (2000). His theory stresses that human's naturally develop reoccurring patterns. However, through getting in touch with the unconscious and identifying unmet needs or inner wounds, buried emotions emerge to the surface. A person may begin to weep about things that happened to them earlier in life.

This happened to me after several Breathwork sessions. I remember it well because it was one of the only times I could express my anger. My emotions took over me and I began hitting the floor and kicking the wall. It started out subtly until one of the main facilitators came over and pulled me back so as not to put a whole in the wall. This triggered an immense surge of rage and I started screaming and kicking uncontrollably. It seemed like my whole body was jerking and in a craze. This lasted almost an hour and I remember I was exhausted afterwards. It was a profound session for me because I was finally able to get in touch with my inner anger and express it in a safe and supportive setting.

In another Breathwork session, I was able to identify with the sacral chakra in a more sensual way. I was moving my body in a circular motion and feeling the rhythm of the music. My "altered state of conscious" had no thought of looking "sexy" to others in the room—it felt good to experience my innate sensuality. Later that day, after the Breathwork session, my roommate and I were having a casual conversation when she said to me, "Wow, you were looking pretty sexy in your Breathwork today." I was unaware of how I looked because I was experiencing an inner feeling. On the outside, she thought I looked promiscuous. Her comment made me wonder if she was inferring that I intended to look provocative or further, that I should feel ashamed.

There is a description of the unconscious realms given by Carl Jung in the book, *Psychology of the Kundalini.* He is describing the symbolism of the water element in reference to the sacral chakra. He calls it the "baptismal fount" containing the danger of the devouring sea. Going into the unconscious he says, "Desire, passions and the whole emotional world breaks loose. Sex, power and every devil in our nature gets loose when we become acquainted with the unconscious" (1996). He adds that one will all of a sudden see a new picture of him or herself.

My "new picture" was temporarily deflated by my roommate's comment. Fortunately, I got over that and welcomed any connection with my body. Our society puts so many constraints on how we should look, feel and behave. According to Inanna's story, we are primal, sexual beings and although it is important to be conscious of our actions and motivations, it is still our human right to express our sexual nature. This connects us to our sacral chakra energy.

The sacral chakras element is water. Water is a symbol of human consciousness. Jung adds that the reason people are afraid of going into the "sea" of the unconscious is because they don't want to know what is lurking in the unconscious mind. People generally prefer to be hidden from dark realms of the psyche. He quotes:

> That is why people are afraid and say there is no unconscious, like children playing hide and seek. A child hides behind a door and says, "Nobody is behind this door; don't look here!" And so we have two marvelous psychological theories that nothing is behind this door, don't look here, this is nothing important. Then you make abstractions, you make marvelous abstract signs of it, and talk of it with only a sort of shy hinting...As sailors never dared to say, "This damned hell of a sea, this black sea that is always so stormy and smashes our ships!" They said, "The welcoming benevolent sea"...in order not to arouse those alarming impressions or to irritate those dark sea demons (1945).

I think it is fair to say that most people still prefer to live at this level of consciousness. They do not wish to go into the "sea", their inner consciousness, and admit to "possessing or entertaining demons." From a different perspective, those demons are only what we call them out to be. In other words, it depends on one's perception of evil.

In his lecture, Jung continues to say, "So it is just that...after baptism you get right into hell." The sacral chakra fuels the energy upward to the brilliant, yellow solar plexus. "From one spectrum it can be seen as the fullness of jewels that manifests out of desire and passion. On the other side it can be viewed as lust, power and greed" (1996). In order to understand the inner consciousness of our psyche, we must recognize we are susceptible to both sides of the spectrum.

This chapter emphasizes humanity's feelings and emotions. It also points out that we are conscious beings.

From a holistic perspective, the range of our existence depends on opposing forces. Everything has an opposite and that includes our conscious and unconscious mind. There is a huge benefit to being aware of these opposing forces and allowing them instead of living a life in denial or as if this range does not exist.

In the next chapter, we will continue with Enki and Inanna's celebration. Enki freely gives Inanna the powers of civilization—the universal laws. This part of her story identifies with the solar plexus chakra's energy which has to do with "the fullness of jewels" and life empowerment.

# Chapter Four –
# **The Boat of Plenty**

*The Fire is one, Bird beating red wings in each thing*
*I am not a voice, I am the Fire singing*
*What you hear is crackling in you.*
*All my splendor is to burn within you*
*To know this Fire that eats me*
*Is eating itself, to be this Fire*
*You brought me Eternal Light*
*In your body's burning cup*
*Laughing as I drank*
*And grew wings of Fire.*
*~Rumi*


*The God of Wisdom swaying with drink, toasted Inanna:*
*"In the name of my holy power! In the name of my holy shrine!*
*To my daughter Inanna I shall give*
*The high priesthood! Godship!*
*The noble, enduring crown! The throne of kingship!"*

*Inanna replied:*
*"I take them!"*

*Enki raised his cup and toasted Inanna again:*
*"In the name of my holy power! In the name of my holy shrine!*
*To my daughter I shall give Truth!*
   *Descent into the underworld! Ascent from the underworld!*
   *The holy priestess of heaven, the setting of lamentations,*
   *The rejoicing of the heart, the art of lovemaking,*
   *The giving of judgments, the making of decisions,*
   *The universal laws and a list of holy decrees.*

*Inanna replied:*
   *"I take them!"*

*(still reeling with drink) Enki spoke to his servant Isimud:*
   *"My sukkal, the young woman is about to leave.*
   *It is my wish that she reach her city safely."*

*Inanna gathered the holy me and placed them on the Boat of*
*Heaven.*
*She pushed off from the quay.*

When the beer had gone out from the God of Wisdom
He looked around and called to his servant,
  "My sukkal, Isimud—
  Where is the noble enduring crown, the high priesthood?"
Isimud replies, "the king has given them to his daughter"
Enki asks once more:
  "The art of lovemaking, the giving of judgments,
  The making of decisions,
  Where are they?"
Again, Isimud replies,
  "My king has given them to his daughter
  My king has given the holy me to his daughter."

Then Enki spoke, saying:
  "Isimud, the Boat of Heaven, the holy me
  Where is it now?
The Boat of Heaven has just left.
Enki orders Isimud:
  "Go! Take the enkum-creatures
  Let them bring the Boat of Heaven back to Eridu!"

Isimud spoke to Inanna:
  "My queen, your father has sent me to you.
Your father's words are words of state.
They may not be disobeyed."

Inanna answered:
"What has my father said?
What are his words of state that may not be disobeyed?"

Isimud spoke:
"My King has said; Let Inanna proceed to Erech
Bring the Boat of Heaven with the holy me back to Eridu."

Inanna cried:
"My father has changed his word to me!
My father has violated his pledge—broken his promise!
Deceitfully he sent you to me!

When Inanna spoke these words
The wild-haired, enkum-creatures seized the Boat of Heaven.

Inanna called to her servant, Ninshubur, saying:
"Ninshubur, once you were Queen of the East
Now you are the faithful servant of the holy shrine of Erech
Water has not touched your hand,

*Water has not touched your foot.*
*My sukkal, who gives me wise advice,*
*My warrior who fights by my side,*
*Save the Boat of Heaven with the holy me!"*
*(Ninshubur sliced the air with her hand. She uttered an earth-*
*shattering cry and the enkum-creatures were motioned away)*

*Seven times Enki sent Isimud to bring back the Boat of Heaven,*
*Seven times Ninshubur rescued the boat for Inanna.*

*Finally, at the seventh gate, the holy me were unloaded.*
*As the universal laws were unloaded,*
*They were announced and presented to the people of Sumer.*

*More laws appeared than what Enki had given Inanna*
*Inanna brought allure, the art of women and perfect execution*
*She brought the drums and the art of ritual and ceremony.*
*Inanna brought the placing of the garment on the ground*

*Lastly, Enki spoke to Inanna, saying:*
        *"In the name of my holy power!*
        *In the name of my holy shrine!*
        *Let the me you have taken with you*
        *remain in the holy shrine of your city.*
        *Let the high priest and priestess*
        *spend their days at the holy shrine in song.*
        *Let the citizens of your city prosper,*
        *Let the children of Erech rejoice.*
        *Let the city of Erech be restored to its great place."*

The pure Inanna follows her inner guidance and travels to visit with her Father Enki, God of the Wisdom. They share their excitement about the over-flowing waters of life. This ritual purification sets the stage for Inanna to be presented the holy me and the powers of civilization. These powers are considered essential to understanding the relationship between man and God and Enki knows that the connection to higher knowledge is vital to the development of civilization.

### She Is Presented the Holy Me

Enki is generous—while in an altered state he freely shares his powers and listens to his inner guidance. He knows the importance of passing on the gifts of civilization to his next worthy kin. Inanna understands the importance of attaining these gifts from her father. The intention of her journey is to be "fertilized" by the magical, spiritual and cultural powers of life and she accomplishes this mission (Wolkstein & Kramer, 1983). Her Father gives her the holy me and she loads the scrolls onto her boat. Inanna is probably in her mid-twenties in this part of the story and she is on fire! She has energy. More important, she is empowered with "the fullness of jewels."

Inanna recognizes her full potential at this stage and she is fearless and determined to succeed. Her mission and purpose definitely includes the people of Sumer. Her desire and passion involve bringing prosperity to the land. As Queen of Heaven and Earth, Inanna wants her city to be full and prosperous. She is on a mission to create civilization in Sumer and she is not willing to let anything get in her way.

Inanna did not expect her father to take back the gifts. She instinctively stands her ground and reaches for her personal power. With a focus on her mission, she reaches for the vitality within her to make it happen. Her energy produces action swiftly because she represents a healthy vessel. She is not afraid to say "no" to her father. She is strong, powerful and focused on what she wants. She says "yes!" to her raw feminine vitality and calls on her spiritual guide for support. Joining with a spiritual force, Inanna does not waver. When she arrives in Erech to unload the gifts, Inanna presents more than was given to her. Not only is she given all the powers of civilization, she is blessed with gifts of the feminine. Inanna arrives with the art of allure and the art of woman. She unloads drums to create the art of ritual and ceremony.

Inanna does not question her decision to keep the holy me. Having a healthy and open sacral chakra, she is gifted with "the making of decisions" and moves into this relationship testing her inner power. This sense of empowerment is evident in the solar plexus chakra of the body which is responsible for helping us make decisions (Myss, 2000). It is here that we take action and use our power to fuel the outcome of whatever choices we make. Making life decisions can be difficult. However, if we make a firm decision about something and follow through it is because of willpower.

### The Solar Plexus Action

The solar plexus chakra's element is fire. Fire fuels the action into igniting and manifesting personal power. The support of a solid base and the flow of the sacral chakra helps ignite the fuel to make things happen and to get the job done. The strength and ability to make decisions is a product of our will that perceives, believes and takes action. The solar plexus energy is where a person has the power to live their life passionately and can manifest their life purpose. The action towards that vision is amplified with healthy solar plexus energy. In *The Psychology of Kundalini Yoga*, Carl Jung tells us:

> There is the source of the fire; there is the fullness of energy! A man or woman who is not on fire is nothing! He is ridiculous; he is two-dimensional. He must be on fire even if he does make a fool of himself. A flame must burn somewhere, otherwise no light shines. There is no warmth, nothing. It is terribly awkward; it is painful, full of conflict, apparently a mere waste of time— at all events, it is against reason. But that accursed Kundalini says, it is the fullness of jewels; there is the source of energy and as Heraclitus aptly said: war is the father of all things (1932).

Jung also references the Buddha, saying "the whole world is in flames, your ears, and your eyes, everywhere you pour out the fire of desire, and that is the fire of illusion because you desire things which are futile" (1932). Jung knew that there was great treasure in releasing emotional energy through the solar plexus element of fire. The solar plexus chakra liberates us to create our life whatever way we want (Davies, 2000).

The fire element will burn through any blockages— including our ego to purify us. Fire stands for cleansing and purification (Fillmore, 2005). It represents revelation, transformation and regeneration (Tresidder, 2000). Also, fire represents the positive, affirming state of mind. We are given the ability to believe in our self. It is here we are able to say yes or no and to act. We are awakened with purpose, strength and will.

The solar plexus chakra allows us to blossom forth and find our purpose in life. This is where we find the strength for inspiration, inner balance and determination. Donna Eden, a modern day energy healer, says,

> The ball of fire heats up our sense of power. It helps center us. The power center is associated with autonomy and sense of self. When this chakra is open, we feel worthy of all that life has to offer us. We realize the power we possess to create the life of our dreams is already alive inside of us. When we harness the energy of our solar plexus, we find the strength to conquer our dreams and goals (2008).

This sense of personal power and self-esteem comes from the interior of the soul, an innate and organic nature, rather than an outward egoic fixation to be seen or controlled.

Inanna shines the light on herself, owns her femininity and embodies a "Here I Am" attitude. She is ready, her energy is open and she is forthright in achieving her mission. We draw from our solar plexus chakra when we have the persistence to keep going despite difficult life circumstances. This chakra allows us to live with tenacity. Inanna is swift in her action and easily endures the challenge of this energy. Brenda Davies says, "the power of the solar plexus chakra gives us unlimited possibilities ~ to work, to create change, to become what we want to be, to realize our ambitions, to be happy, to drive our lives wherever we want to go" (2000). The solar plexus chakra gives us the ability to take action.

If this chakra is out of balance an unfortunate picture ensues. We may feel like frustrated victims of circumstance. Enki's actions are a good example of this. He fumbles to get back what he so freely and happily gave away the day before. In his drunken stupor, he presents the holy me to the lovely Inanna. As soon as the drink wears off, Enki awakens to the realization that he gave away the Divine decrees. He reacts immediately and changes his manner to that of a victim. He instructs Isimud to send forth the sea monsters and seize the Boat of Heaven—filled with the powers of civilization—to bring back to Eridu. Enki's dark side emerges and he becomes the opposite of a joyous, generous and loving father. After giving away the holy me and then regretting his decision, Enki behaves like the dark shaman who withholds rather than gives (Wolkstein and Kramer, 1983).

### The Dark Shaman

Enki's actions remind us of the importance of boundaries. It is important to recognize and establish good boundaries before we give things away too easily. If we find ourselves in situations unable to say no and then later regretting it—we should consider that we don't have good boundaries. We often see the dark shaman lurking in our society today. For example, look at the recent disaster of our banking industry. This recent movement was unlike anything we ever experienced in history. People were able to get loans for homes as long as their credit was good and as long as they had a required down payment. This was the first time the banks had loosened the reigns for home loans. Then the real estate industry skyrocketed and the value of homes reached an all-time high. Unfortunately, many homeowners couldn't afford the increased property taxes and other mandatory expenses, like insurance, that went along with the cost of owning a home. It wasn't long before people were defaulting on their loans and the banks were asking for a bail out. This is a good example to show the importance of having good boundaries to prevent future turmoil and chaos.

When the solar plexus chakra is out of sorts we may feel like our integrity is compromised and we react by making excuses or projecting blame on others. Enki's reaction appears defensive when he calls on the sea monsters to bring back the holy me. Enki, the God of Wisdom, is apparently acting out of his ego when he unexpectedly orders his servant to find Inanna and return the powers of civilization. This scene becomes increasingly tense.

Enki does not relent until Inanna has reached the seventh gate. This action on Enki's part easily reflects our own intensity when we become antagonistic. This can be representative of our own defensive nature and unwillingness to give our power away. If we can be honest with ourselves and recognize this reaction, we can learn so much from it. The truth is we don't usually want to face our own shortcomings. However, with willpower, good intentions and the ability to surrender to one's inner defense, the promise for a higher level of consciousness is sure to be attained.

The solar plexus chakras opposite spectrum can be perceived as the power hungry ego. In Philip Shepherd's, *New Self, New World*, he describes the power hungry ego and the cycle of turmoil one may undergo:

> The fears that have centered us in our heads are the fears that create the tyrant; and the central fear that creates the tyrant is a fear of the female: the tyrant segregates himself from the uncontrollable vagaries of being and seeks always to fortify what is 'mine', intent on preserving it from a world of ceaseless change. Whenever that fantasy of what is rightfully 'his' is at odds with the world, he will seek to arrest or subjugate the world, just as he has subjugated the body. The willfulness or even...a willingness to subjugate is the basic impulse of

64

tyranny. That potential is alive in each of us, and will spring forth whenever we heed will above world – for such an allegiance blinds us to 'what is', even as it blinds us to the vanities of entitlement. The tyrant is self-serving, and his personal mission is to distort his being to support the fantasy of his personal power (2010).

This sense of autocracy or domination pertains to men and women alike. Women can feel as if they are refuting their own desires and emotions to be strong for others. They eventually become offensive and show outbursts of anger and resentment.

When confronted with human problems, force will not bring a lasting solution. This is what I read recently from the Dalai Lama. He wants us to know that his Holiness attaches great importance to the feeling of mutual love among all human beings, as well as to the sense of responsibility of community life (2011). The Dalai Lama believes these concepts are the source of peace everywhere in the world. They are the origin of all individual and collective fulfillment in a human community and therefore of concern to us all.

This is our ideal trajectory and one in which we all have the potential to create. Through awakening to our attachments, be it emotional or material, we have a better chance of reaching our highest potential in life which correlates with the upward flow of energy through the chakras. This also requires a healthy and open heart chakra along with a willingness to be present and aware of all things.

### Queen of the East

Inanna recognizes the dual nature of her father and takes action. She calls on her spiritual servant, Ninshubur, or Queen of the East, who carries powers of the sun that quench those of the water. This is Inanna's messenger and protector. The Queen of the East is symbolic of a ray of sunlight representing an eternal flame. This is a

65

masculine and active element symbolizing both creative and destructive energy.

Carl Jung explains his idea of calling for Divine assistance and guidance through identification with the solar plexus chakra:

> This is where one becomes part of the divine substance, having an immortal soul. You are already part of that which is no longer in time, 3-dimensional space; you belong now to a four-dimensional order of things where time is only an extension, where space does not exist and time is not, where there is only infinite duration— eternity (1932).

The underlying force to create change lies in the power of transformation.

The Queen of the East assists Inanna in her mission to bring the powers of civilization to Erech through a symbolic baptism. Again, we can refer to Jung's depiction of the solar plexus chakra. He explains that "the light comes after the baptism, the deification that always follows the baptismal rite" (1932). Inanna's initiation, her baptismal fount, is evident and further emphasized by the passing through of seven ports.

Ninshubur assists Inanna through seven stopping points between Eridu and Erech where the sea monsters are ready to seize the Boat of Heaven at each port. Inanna's determination is relentless, and through her spiritual servants' power, she defeats Enki's sea monsters. By doing this, she obtains the God of Wisdom's shamanic powers. Therefore, she returns to her city not only representing the Hero but the Shaman as well. Wolkstein tells us in *Inanna, Queen of Heaven and Earth* that hero's wrestle the treasure from the adversary—shamans use higher powers to protect the well-being of people. Inanna offers to her people that which will nourish them both physically and spiritually.

Another angle to this story is that Inanna could be acting out of anger and frustration. Women who have unconscious resentment may react with stubbornness, control and/or spite. Women crave a sense of self-worth and identity too. Recognizing these deep inner emotions helps us connect with inner confidence and self-esteem.

When not acknowledged, women are just as likely as men to respond with malice and react unconsciously. The myth of *The Handless Maiden* written by Robert Johnson, a famous Jungian analyst, can be used to explain why women have lost their self-worth.

In the story, Johnson explains we have sold our feeling sense, a feminine aspect, for machines and the ability to produce more. One of the main characters is a farmer who makes a deal with the devil to buy machinery for his farm which will enable him to make a lot more money. When his payment comes due, he realizes it is in exchange for his daughter. The farmer doesn't want to surrender his daughter or his riches so he does as the devil requests and cuts off her hands instead. Hence, she is the handless maiden without any feeling sense. Unfortunately, this story is a realistic metaphor for what has happened with women and our society as a whole. The current problem we are now faced with is how it is affecting our children in regard to video games.

In our modern times, it is common for two parents to bring in an income. Unless the children are in school while the parents are working, they are brought to a pre-school. As teenagers, they are home alone. Some families need both parents to work in order to pay the bills. But many parents are unconsciously motivated by "having it all" or as the modern saying goes, "keeping with the Jones." Children desperately need their parents love and attention and will react with unconscious motives to get that attention. Often times this becomes a vicious cycle of the child getting whatever they want.

Kids don't need that much in terms of material possessions, they are happy to play outside and keep it simple. However, the electronics industry has infiltrated our children's lives convincing them they need these things. As parents, we are ultimately responsible because of two main reasons: 1) parents are busy doing too many things so they buy video games to pacify their child's attention and 2) children watch too much television which exposes them to commercials or subliminal marketing. Too much television and/or video games suppresses children's connection with the physical world which in turn can create low self-esteem. This can easily trickle into adulthood and create imbalances in their future goals and aspirations.

When will we recognize that "we have sold our feeling sense" so we can have more unnecessary material possessions? In most cases, possessions and having more "stuff" does not satisfy our human needs. We are already recognizing this truth based on the status of our economy. Many people are experiencing a cleansing or refining of attachments to material things. This is not as much a Baptism as it is what Jung calls, "a purification by fire." This represents our current economic crisis and the tragic losses that ensued in western civilization resulting from our sense of greed and power. In general, we are all undergoing a shift of priorities resulting from a collective desire to have more material things.

### Validation and Responsibility

In Inanna's story, she is first gifted with the holy me. Then her father tries to take back the gifts. At first her father acknowledges her, but then she must take action for herself. Inanna is forthright and steadfast. She takes a stand and validates her self-worth. Further, she does so for the well-being of others.

In our society today, it is common for women to expect men to validate them. That is all well and good but men typically validate from a masculine energy—through objects, adoration and possessions. There is nothing wrong with this unless it turns into a barter and reduces our self-esteem.

Women validate themselves and each other from a feminine perspective. Women are more likely than men to validate another's feelings. Women are more apt to accommodate others and show nurturance. Inanna calls on her feminine spiritual servant—her power within—for help. All women have this power; we just need to get in touch with it. Encompassing awareness or a shift toward our feminine inner energy will ignite the light within and help us recognize this inner power.

Abraham Maslow, a lead scholar in Humanistic Psychology, believes that every person has a strong desire to reach his or her full potential which signifies a level of self-actualization (1968). At this level, humans are not blindly reacting to situations but trying to accomplish something greater. All human beings have the capacity to fulfill his or her life's purpose and mission. Maslow describes this as "reaching one's highest potential."

Inanna's story, written thousands of years ago, delivers the message that we all are capable of reaching our highest potential and obtaining empowerment. It is only a matter of believing in our self and owning our inner strength (i.e., willpower). Inanna makes an effort to relate to the people of her city and encourages them to blossom forth and flourish.

### Real Confidence

Inanna's determination and willpower to fulfill her life's purpose reflects strength. I can relate to this determination in my own life. Since I was seventeen, I have been setting goals. So far, I have been able to accomplish or complete what I set out to do. This has never been the problem.

In order to fully potentiate the energy in my solar plexus chakra, I had to do some healing work with my root and sacral chakra. My self-esteem was missing and it wasn't until I went through a really tough period in my life that I realized what was wrong. It was easy for me to get good grades, to keep appointments and to walk around with a big smile on my face but inside I didn't believe in my self. As I got older, I learned that believing in my self was the most important achievement I can attain. I realized that achievements don't mean anything if I am not confident or self-possessed.

Through my life example, it is easy to see when one has areas in their life that have not been healed or are unhealthy. My issue centered on believing in my self. My unconscious ego took over at times and led me to believe I wasn't important. I fortunately overcame this pattern and emerged with the awareness I needed to continue forward on my mission.

What do I accredit my newfound confidence to? Toastmasters International, a non-profit organization, designed to help people become better communicators. This is inclusive of both speaking and listening. It works and it is the best thing I ever did for my self-esteem.

Speaking in front of an audience sounds more like it has to do with communication or the throat chakra, but until someone has inner confidence, they will not be able to find their voice and project it. I decided to boost my confidence even more and ran for President of my Toastmaster club. I heard the call and knew it would be good for me to confront my fear. After I signed up and was voted in, I questioned my decision. All of my fears began to surface. I was terrified of how people would judge me and kept saying to myself, "What am I doing?" but I stayed with my instinct and before long I became comfortable and worthy of my position as President of the club. Beyond that, I decided to start a women's networking group in my local neighborhood. I finally felt a sense of inner confidence. I believed in my self and my leadership qualities.

This business women's group, called Women on a Mission, meets every other week for lunch. When we meet, we share goals and aspirations; we support each other. We gather together not only to acknowledge each other but we strive to empower each other! This group of women is growing rapidly which signifies there is a need for this type of communing between women. We have a greater capacity to feel empowered and heal ourselves through the support of a group.

### Weighing the Consequence

One of the best ways a woman can heal herself is to seek the support of another woman. Inanna immediately calls for support when she is faced with adversity. Strong female leaders are a great example of empowerment and inspiration. Women who organize support groups or community service events lead a good example as well.

Women who are leaders in their community have healthy solar plexus energy. With a positive trajectory, we can overcome obstacles that keep us victimized and catatonic. If the solar plexus energy is blocked or unhealthy, the trajectory does not flow forward into the heart chakra as is intended. It stays in the lower chakras.

A great way to describe this concept is an excerpt out of Joseph Campbell's book, *The Inner Reaches of Outer Space*. He refers to *The Book of the Dead* and the Egyptian judgment scene where, upon death, one undergoes a process of having one's heart weighed against a feather. The "Swallower" is to eat the soul if the heart weighs heavier than the feather. Campbell says, "In terms of the Kundalini, the message could hardly be clearer; namely, if the aims of the [one who is] deceased...were no higher than those of chakra 3, the Swallower claims the soul" (1986). Campbell continues to explain that if the feather is not outweighed, the blessed soul will be welcomed to Osiris's throne by the Waters of Eternal Life.

> The Egyptian feather against which the heart of the deceased was to be weighted was an ostrich feather symbolic of the goddess Maat, as a personification of the cosmic order and its natural laws, to which both the social order and the order of an individual lifetime were required to conform (1986).

There are many people in today's society unaware of this "rite of passage" and prefer not to identify with their heavy heart. Therefore, their energy—or their soul—never

71

reaches the upward flow through the heart and head chakras as was intended from the Egyptian Gods.

In order for our modern human society to evolve we will need to overextend ourselves and start acting responsibly. We all have been wounded and victimized at one point or another and will easily claim that role but we rarely claim to be the perpetrator. Manjushri, the Buddha that cuts away illusion, teaches us that we are all capable of being the perpetrator and the victim. In the final story of Manjushri's power, he says:

> Once five hundred monks were able to see their pasts, and discovered that they had all killed their own parents or committed other atrocities. They came to doubt that they would ever achieve enlightenment. Sensing this, the Buddha called on Manjushri to instruct them. [He] instantly pulled out his sword and placed it at the Buddha's neck. The monks [understood] his point: the mind is illusory. There is no sword, no Buddha, no Manjushri-therefore there were no crimes, no criminals, no victims. With his sword of truth Manjushri cut through the illusion and showed them reality as it really is.      (Mybuddhadharma. blogspot.com, 2010)

Women have played the role of victim for thousands of years, but it is time for them to face the call and heal these inner wounds. Women are being summoned to take the lead in society through business, community service and as an empowered female in the family household. Now is the time for all women, even women that feel sorry for themselves, to stop blaming others. If we all took a look within and did some inner healing, we can heal our issues around forgiveness, anger and resentment.

If the female race can show up as empowered, instead of useless victims of chance, it is more likely they will be respected as the nurturers and healers of the world. If women can move forward into the heart space and seek forgiveness, they are very likely to evolve into a new world order. This would allow all of us, the entire human race, to open our hearts, to seek forgiveness and to see the Divine in every one.

In the next chapter, we will explore the love in our hearts and how to find forgiveness in others and in our self. It is time for a change in our collective conscious. This change will encompasses love, compassion and a devout service to humanity as a whole. Inanna has every intention of belonging to another and experiencing union with her beloved Dumuzi. Through mirroring her lover, Inanna discovers love is blissful. The next part of Inanna's story shares the most wonderful time in her life. She meets her significant other, Dumuzi, and they quickly announce their plans for marriage.

# Chapter Five –
## The Sacred Marriage Ritual

*While the image of the Beloved burns in our heart
the whole of life flows in contemplation.
Wherever union with the Beloved exists
there is, in the middle of the house,
a flowering rose garden.
~Rumi*

*The brother spoke to his younger sister.
The Sun God, Utu, spoke to Inanna, saying:
Young lady, the flax in its fullness is lovely.
Inanna, the grain is glistening in the furrow.
I will hoe it for you, I will bring it to you.
Inanna spoke:
Brother, after you've brought the flax
Who will comb it for me?
Sister, I will bring it to you combed.
Who will spin it for me?
Sister, I will bring it to you spun.
Who will braid and warp it for me?
Sister, I will bring it to you braided and warped.
Who will weave it and bleach it for me?
Brother, after you've brought my bridal sheet to me,
Who will go to bed with me?*

*Sister, your bridegroom will go to bed with you.
Dumuzi, the shepherd, he will go to bed with you
Inanna spoke:
No, brother! The man of my heart works the hoe
The farmer! He is the man of my heart!
He gathers the grain into great heaps.
He brings the grain regularly into my storehouses.*

*Sister, marry the shepherd.
Why are you unwilling?
Dumuzi will share his rich cream with you
You who are meant to be the King's protector*

*Inanna spoke:
The shepherd! I will not marry the shepherd!
His clothes are coarse; his wool is rough.
I will marry the farmer.*

*The farmer grows flax for my clothes.*
*The farmer grows barley for my table.*

*Dumuzi spoke:*
*Why do you speak about the farmer?*
*If he gives you black flour,*
*I will give you black wool,*
*If he gives you beer,*
*I will give you sweet milk.*
*If he gives you bread,*
*I will give you honey cheese.*
*I will give the farmer my leftover cream.*

*Dumuzi went to the royal house with milk.*
*Before the door, he called out:*
*Open the house, my Lady, open the house!*

*Inanna ran to Ningal, her mother who bore her.*
*Ningal counseled her daughter,*
*The young man will be your father, your mother*
*He will treat you as a father and care for you like a mother*

*At her mother's command,*
*Inanna bathed and anointed her self with scented oil.*
*She covered her body with the royal white robe.*
*She arranged her precious lapis beads around her neck.*
*Dumuzi waited expectantly.*

*Inanna opened the door for him.*
*Inside the house she shone before him*
*Like the light of the moon.*
*Dumuzi looked at her joyously.*
*He pressed his neck close against her and kissed her.*

*Inanna spoke:*
*What I tell you let the singer weave into song.*
*What I tell you, let it flow from your ear to mouth,*
*Let it pass from old to young.*
*My vulva, the horn, the Boat of Heaven*
*Is full like the eagerness of the young moon*
*My untilled land lies fallow.*

*As for me, Inanna*
*Who will plow my vulva?*
*Who will plow my high field?*
*Who will plow my wet ground?*

*As for me, the young woman*
*Who will plow my vulva?*
*Who will station the ox there?*
*Who will plow my vulva?*

*Dumuzi replied:*
*"Great Lady, the King will plow your vulva*
*I, Dumuzi the King, will plow your vulva*

*At the king's lap stood the rising cedar.*
*Plants grew high by their side.*
*Grains grew high by their side.*
*Gardens flourished luxuriantly.*

*Inanna sang:*
*He has sprouted; he has burgeoned;*
*He is lettuce planted by the water.*
*He is the one my womb loves best.*
*My well-stocked garden of the plain*
*My barley growing high in its furrow*
*My apple tree which bears fruit up to its crown,*
*He is lettuce planted by the water.*

*My honey-man, my honey-man sweetens me always.*
*My lord, the honey-man of the gods,*
*He is the one my womb loves best.*
*His hand is honey, his foot is honey and he sweetens me always.*

*My eager impetuous caresser of the navel,*
*My caresser of the soft thighs,*
*He is the one my womb loves best,*

*Dumuzi sang:*
*O lady your breast is your field,*
*Inanna, your breast is your field.*
*Your broad field pours out plants.*
*Your broad field pours out grain.*
*Water flows from on high for your servant.*
*Bread flows from on high for your servant.*
*Pour it out for me, Inanna.*
*I will drink all you offer.*

*Inanna sang:*
*Make your drink sweet and thick, my bridegroom.*
*My shepherd, I will drink your fresh milk.*
*Wild bull, Dumuzi, make your milk sweet and thick.*

*Let the milk of the goat flow in sheepfold.*
*Fill my holy churn with honey cheese.*
*Lord Dumuzi, I will drink your fresh milk.*

*My husband, I will guard my sheepfold for you.*
*I will watch over your house of life, the storehouse,*
*The shining quivering place which delights Sumer—*
*It is this house which decides the fate of the land,*
*It is this house which gives the breath of life to the people.*
*I, the Queen of the Palace, will watch over your house.*


An important Goddess of the ancient Near East, Inanna was recognized as the Goddess of Love and Fertility. Dumuzi and Inanna come together in this romantic telling of a springtime love affair. The love and union of Dumuzi and Inanna symbolizes the joy of the heart. They come together as opposites and unite as one. By taking all their nourishment from each other, each becomes in turn parent and child, feeder and fed (Wolkstein & Kramer, 1983).

Utu, Inanna's brother, is clear in his message that the time is ripe for Inanna to find a mate. He calls her the King's protector. When Dumuzi and Inanna meet, her untilled land lies fallow. She is missing a very important piece of her growth, to be filled by another. The sacred marriage ritual in Sumeria was performed in the springtime. Springtime is the time of regeneration, fertility and renewal. It is the time of new beginnings.

### An Ancient Ritual

The sacred marriage ritual is about growth and rebirth. It is about producing prosperity in the land or the country in which it is enacted. In ancient Mesopotamia, this was expressed through a ritual, called the Sacred Marriage ritual, and it was performed every year for centuries. The high priestess embodied the Goddess, most known as Ishtar (Ishtar is the Babylonian image of Inanna).

Through ritual and ceremony they consummated a union symbolizing fertility across the land. In the Babylonian era, King Solomon built a temple for Ishtar to venerate her and to honor this sacred ritual. This ceremony was an expression of the gratitude and respect to the God and Goddess. The people were rewarded for celebrating the union of masculine and feminine through the blessings of fertility and prosperity.

In the start of this passage, Inanna is determined to marry the farmer. Her brother, Utu, sees things differently. He sees that Inanna is better suited with the shepherd, a guide, someone to steer the flock in order to get the best outcome for Erech. Inanna is resistant at first but when she meets Dumuzi and senses his embodiment of power and strength, she starts to change her mind.

Dumuzi represents himself with fortitude and courage. He approaches Inanna and is determined to win her over. Perhaps Inanna sees a bit of herself in him and finds him challenging. After a consult with her mother, Inanna decides to "open her house" to Dumuzi. He has succeeded in winning her over. He is bringing something "to the table." In fact, he is bringing more than Inanna had hoped for. Inanna notices something stir within her as her heart opens towards another.

She not only opens her house, she opens her heart as well. The heart is the dwelling place of all our vulnerable and human encounters. With an open heart, we are compassionate and we recognize that love is a powerful emotion. Love is the stronghold that drives us. When two people fall in love, they see this shining light and glorious beauty emanating from the other. They express openness for each other that is quite sensual. They are in the "enclosed garden", mirroring each other, and seeking only the joy they exchange. They believe the other is flawless and can do no wrong.

### Foreplay at its Finest

Inanna and Dumuzi express a wonderful exploitation of their intimacy for each other through the symbolism of rising cedar, tall growing plants, luxurious flourishing gardens and the golden flax. In the springtime, we automatically encompass heightened body senses.

Imagine yourself outside in the peak of spring experiencing the sweetness of this magical moment! Inanna starts singing joyously. She uses words of rich symbolism to explain what Dumuzi does for her. He sings back to her, "Inanna your breast is your field. Your broad field pours out grain." Together they are extremely fertile beings and they want to drink and immerse in this love. This eloquent, poetic courtship is filled with blossoming fertility and growth. They taste the desire within and begin to yearn for each other. They allow their bodies to soak in the splendor of this joyous feeling as if they are submerged in the experience of bittersweet bliss!

Inanna represents the feminine and Dumuzi the masculine; they have a healthy desire to integrate the two. The heart chakra is about uniting or harmonizing the opposites. Inanna and Dumuzi create a scene whereby the only possible outcome is peace, harmony, joy and acceptance. They are fully engaged in each other and their hearts are wide open. They sing joyously as they sprout sweet love songs to each other.

Between the two, there is an intermingling of male and female energies: Inanna drinks Dumuzi's milk and he drinks hers (Wolkstein and Kramer, 1983). Inanna will literally be filled with Dumuzi's milk or seed which in turn will sprout prosperity and fullness to all of Erech. The door to each others house is wide open. They call each other brother and sister; terms of affection and kinship in ancient love songs.

Inanna urges the man of her heart to fertilize her— all of her. Her readiness and eagerness incite his energies and Dumuzi blossoms. As soul mates, they wander together in the spring garden of life. Inanna and Dumuzi are interested not only in their own growth but the growth of the city of Erech. Through their connection and their open hearts they pass on the joy they both possess which activates the growth of leadership, strength, guidance and fertility to all of their people.

Inanna asks "who will plow my high field?" We can assume this as an inference to "who will plow my earth?" The yin aspect of nature is the soil, the dirt, the night, the unseen. Dumuzi represents the yang and the upright, the glistening phallus in all its glory and pride. Together, the moist soil and sprouted seed are gorgeous—they signify the harvesting of earth. This can be viewed as a lover and beloved that incorporates a much broader scale and reaches beyond two people. With Inanna and Dumuzi, it is evident that through the beloved, through a union with a counterpart, fertility expands to the land and to the people of Erech.

A wonderful example of this union is the recent royal wedding of Prince William and Katherine. Their courtship incited the people of Britain with great hope. This extended to the whole world. Those who watched the details leading up to the royal wedding and the ceremony, were emotionally touched and filled with encouragement.

Dumuzi has gifts for Inanna and she in turn grants him the kingship and powers of Erech. Inanna calls for the royal bed and commits herself to serving her new husband. Ninshubur, her faithful servant, restates Inanna's pledge in a more public manner: "Inanna, Queen of Heaven and Earth, will empower her husband who will then be titled King and servant of all Sumer and Akkad (Wolkstein & Kramer, 1983). The marriage is consummated and followed by Dumuzi's withdrawal to kingly matters. Unfortunately, like any good love story, this romance often fades.

Inanna finds herself without the attention of her husband and a call to self-exploration instead. Before we explore the depths of Inanna's journey, a journey that can affect us all, there is much to explore about the heart chakra center. This chakra can be layers deep and requires a continuous refining. To approach this from a Sufi philosophy (a Middle Eastern spiritual path), the connection to one's beloved requires a continuous polishing of the heart.

### Opening the Layers of the Heart Chakra

Having an open heart is the key to living a joyous life but it requires a positive outlook and finding joy in all things. This place of love and bliss can be experienced all the time but be cautioned that it can also become a false sense of

81

identity. Some great mystics and saints actually do feel this way all the time. Rumi, the ancient Sufi mystic and poet, describes this as being in love with his beloved. This beloved is in everyone and in the whole universe too. But not everybody realizes that reaching this level of the heart chakra is very sacred and requires peeling away layers of hurt and old wounds. The ability to live each moment as if it were a delightful union in the holy gardens sounds possible, but not everyone can stay there.

In reality, we are all struggling and getting by the best we can. As soon as we think "this is the epidemy" we are met with disappointment. But heartbreak allows us to open our hearts even more. We may either experience heartbreak personally or know someone who has. The important thing to remember is that it can be a catalyst for transformation.

We are able to change our perspective and see that all human beings suffer. In the heart chakra, this suffering is met with open arms and comes from a place of gratitude instead of feeling like a victim. This transforms into a deeper compassion for others. If we experience this early in life, we learn to surrender.

The healthy, open heart chakra gives one the ability to love unconditionally and to let go of resentment. This is the same love that Jesus teaches us in scripture; his message tells us "Do unto others what you would want done unto yourself." We are guided by this powerful message to take a look within and surrender to our ego. If the lower chakras are healthy and developed, it is easier to let go of dislikes or judgments.

On the other hand, if the heart space is not open a person can unconsciously act out of bitterness and react with feelings of jealousy, envy or personal contempt. If one is strong enough to recognize these feelings, they can change their perspective and begin to appreciate the real joy of having an open heart chakra.

To stay empowered, a person must also develop and identify with the principle of non-attachment. In other words, they can let go of the fears that keep them attached to their emotions. This person can look at the situation internally and control his or her actions so as not to hurt or control another. It is not easy to be honest about our self-serving motivations but it is certainly necessary if one is willing to surrender and keep the heart chakra open.

A person who is able to consider others and take a look at their own shortcomings obviously loves with an open heart. This person loves and accepts others beyond their personal emotions and reactivity. When a person is able to surrender to this love, they make choices that do not create blockages between two people but rather opens them. This is similar to the phrase, "when you love something, set it free. If it comes back to you, it is yours. If it doesn't, it never was." Anyone who has the capacity to actually do this is capable of surrendering to their ego. They are also capable of surrendering to God or Divine will. In the book, *Anatomy of the Spirit*, Carolyn Myss, says,

> More than any other chakra, the heart chakra represents our capacity to "let go and let God." With its energy we accept our personal emotional challenges as extensions of a Divine plan, which has as its intent our conscious evolution. By releasing our emotional pain, by letting go of our need to know why things have happened as they have, we reach a state of tranquility. In order to achieve that inner peace...we have to embrace the healing energy of forgiveness and release our lesser need for human, self-determined justice (2000).

Forgiveness and acceptance of others without judgment offers harmony, balance and peace. This peace is felt within but it can also be shared with others.

The heart chakra is where we do things as an act of service and with joy. A good example of this is someone who enjoys doing random acts of kindness. We can also witness these compassionate acts of someone we know and reflect upon the joy he or she feels from being in service.

83

The basic qualities of the heart chakra are love and joy. Tagore, a modern day prophet, said "I slept and dreamt that life was joy. I awoke and saw that life was service. I acted and behold, service was joy." Tagore is a great example of a man who lives with a big open heart.

We may know someone personally who lives their life this way. I was lucky enough to know a man that gave freely from his heart and served others. His name was Tom West and he was an inspiration to many. I will never forget him or the memorial service in his honor. We were all touched by his loving kindness and ability to stay positive and happy despite life's challenges. At his service, his family and friends shared a poem written by Kahlil Gibran called *On Death:*

*You would know the secret of death.*
*But how shall you find it unless you*
*seek it in the heart of life?*
*The owl whose night-bound eyes are blind unto the day*
*cannot unveil the mystery of light.*
*If you would indeed behold the spirit of death,*
*open your heart wide unto the body of life.*
*For life and death are one,*
*even as the river and the sea are one.*
*In the depth of your hopes and desires lies your silent*
*knowledge of the beyond;*
*And like seeds dreaming beneath the snow*
*your heart dreams of spring.*
*Trust the dreams, for in them, is hidden the gate to eternity.*
*Your fear of death*
*is but the trembling of the shepherd*
*when he stands before the king*
*whose hand is to be laid upon him in honor.*
*Is the shepherd not joyful beneath his trembling,*
*that he shall wear the mark of the king?*

### The Joy of the Heart

A person who embraces life challenges is an inspiration to humanity. They see through the heart center of the body. When someone sees the world through the heart chakra center, they recognize that everyone is doing the best they can. Each one of us is dancing our "dance of joy." However, we must be willing to take responsibility and stay awake to our ego. This level of the heart chakra requires a commitment to surrender to the Divine and recognize that we are all part of the same source. As the heart chakra opens wider, one often seeks a spiritual guide or commits their life to be in service for humanity and for their beloved Divine source.

Marianne Woodman, an inspirational author and Jungian analyst, tells us: "As we let our life shine, we consciously give other people permission to do the same. As we are liberated from our own fear, our presence actually liberates others" (1992). What this means is that there is no need to "fix" anyone of their shortcomings; it will happen regardless, but only when they are ready. It is more important that we cultivate own inner healing and allow our own light to shine. One can be available as support for another and listen as a concerned friend. Understanding and compassion for another are great characteristics to behold. If you shy away from someone who is going through a lot of difficulty, keep in mind, it could be you one day. Stay open to lending an ear for another.

A person with a healthy heart chakra is an inspiration for others. People all over the world are creating encouraging and inspirational blogs to share with others. One in particular is called the Ireland Lightworkers. The author shared her description of what love is:

> Love is and can be looked at from an inward perspective. Love is the ultimate mirror. When we love our Self and have looked at what triggers us or why we fall into patterns, we are better able to be compassionate for others. Those others are a reflection of our Self and sometimes teach us huge lessons, children can be a wonderful example of this (2010).

Have you ever thought of love in this way? If you are able to look in the mirror and honestly ask yourself what it is that triggers you, you will most likely see that it is a shadow characteristic of your own.

In the first chapter, I shared a scenario where I chose to ask myself why I continued to allow my son's stepmom to upset me. I repeated a question in my head, "What if I was her?" Instead of continuing on my trajectory and feeding my ego through drama and hatred, I began to get in touch with it. I began to see her through a different lens that led me to feeling compassion for her. I will admit that this was not easy; it took discipline, time and constant reflection. However, this practice served its purpose because my son recognized this shift in me which resulted in him opening his heart to me instead of becoming more resentful.

Loving another becomes evident when we begin to honor each other's shortcomings. Most of the time it is difficult for people to honestly look in the mirror and see their reflection in another. It is easier to keep the blinders on, put the blame on others and react defensively. That is why the divorce rate is the highest it has ever been. Unfortunately, most people aren't interested in honoring this important principle and taking a look within. For those that do, it is vital to spend time alone, nurturing and caring for the self.

The process of waking up or "peeling away another layer of the onion" is a powerful healing process. We can easily become our own worst critic and beat up on our self when we discover we have lived our whole life envious of other people or unconsciously judging others. When this happens, we can feel vulnerable or unstable. The best thing we can do is be nice to our self, as if we were a best friend, instead of acting as a worst enemy.

Self-love and self-acceptance are not easy concepts to grasp. We should be gentle with ourselves when doing inner work and remember that it is a process of unfolding. Inevitably, this will get better as we begin to grow. When we learn to take a look within and reflect love on others (instead of envy or scorn), it returns twofold with a deeper sense of love and compassion for our self. We awaken to self-love through the process of self-discovery. We can also awaken to a deeper self through a connection with the Divine or a beloved source.

Connecting with the Divine can actually lift someone off their feet. This feeling of lightness is similar to the feeling of falling in love. We feel like we are floating or "walking on cloud nine." Carl Jung explains this through the heart chakra's element which is air. This is what gives us that feeling of being lifted up or weightless. Jung's detailed description of "being lifted up" in the heart chakra is extraordinary. His eloquent language allows the reader to dive in and visualize a seemingly intangible concept.

> In anahata (the heart chakra) you behold the *purusa*, a small figure that is the divine self, namely, that which is not identical with mere causality, mere nature, mere release of energy that runs down blindly with no purpose. People lose themselves completely in their emotions and deplete themselves, and finally they are burned to bits. In anahata a new thing comes up, the possibility of lifting himself above the emotional happenings and beholding them. He discovers the *purusa* (self) in his heart. If you succeed in remembering yourself, in making a difference between yourself and that outburst of passion, then you discover the Self (1996).

Jung is referring to individuation and experiencing the higher Self. He adds that when one begins to individuate it is becoming that thing which is not the ego. Jung says, "The ego is always far down in [the root chakra] and suddenly becomes aware of something above in the fourth story [which] is the Self." This higher Self is objective, it is impersonal.

By doing our own inner work, we can take this vertical approach, what Jung calls the purusa, to life and to our own internal process. We can think of life symbolically as a cross or a plus sign. The vertical line is our self, or higher Self, and the horizontal line crossing through the heart center is our ego. The upper chakras are met with the lower, more earthly chakras in the center of the body where our heart chakra energy is located. This energy projects outward to those we love.

If we can let go of judgments or expectations and free our mind from attachments, we are able to live sincerely in this heart space and connect with those around us. We have gone through an individuation of the self. We connect with our Divine source in the upper chakras and the energy comes back around in the heart.

### The True Meaning of the Cross

These two lines of the cross can be considered opposites that meet and unite like the balance of yin and yang or feminine and masculine. We can think of Inanna and Dumuzi intersecting at the midpoint of the cross. They are not only opposites in their physical aspects of masculine vs. feminine, they are opposite in human vs. Divine. In the midstream of Inanna's life, she decides to unite with another and that union begins at the center of the heart. Those who are capable of surrendering can move forward and live in the world with a constant sense of compassion.

In Chapter Four, I shared Campbell's image of the Egyptian judgment scene. The heart chakra is weighed against a feather. Symbolically, if the heart is as light as a feather by the time one dies, he or she is able to move onward. On the other hand, if one carries around a heavy heart their whole life, they signify a person that remains attached to their emotions. They continue to live with a cycle of old belief systems.

What is not evident in this judgment scene from the *Book of the Dead* is the heart chakra holds layers and layers of emotion. From the heart, one will spiral upward through the throat, brow and crown chakras and come around to return once again to the heart chakra, revealing a deeper layer.

The heart chakra is an important part of our life development that continues forward like a trajectory—unfolding over time. This trajectory requires a practice of taking a look within. Humans are the only species on earth capable of this level of compassion and love. But we are only capable of peeling away one layer at a time. If we experience a major loss or trauma, including divorce, we may unconsciously revert back to a previous layer. This is considered a coping mechanism that is perceived by some as "building a wall," "wearing a mask" or being unable to connect with others. These actions are all part of the heart center and represent a person's resistance to vulnerability.

If we come up through the lower three centers and are fortunate to have been exposed to positive experiences and healthy outcomes, our heart space will continue to remain open. We can be fully present in the moment and embrace the full peak of joy that life brings. Like springtime gives us that aliveness and full range of all our senses, so to does the experience of being in love.

Repeated unhealthy experiences of life can lessen our chance of looking at shortcomings. Many times people blame others for their unhappiness, misfortune or lack of feeling loved. This outweighs the chance of going inward and taking a look in the mirror. Staying awake to projection and controlling judgmental thoughts makes it much easier to harness a positive outlook and to let go of a co-dependent nature that keeps us in this downward spiraling pattern.

### Letting Go

In the heart chakra, we begin to understand our attachment to others. It is important to recognize that we need our loved ones. Our family, friends, spouses and lovers are important and interdependent to our survival. We naturally love our fellow human counterparts and we logically feel attached to them. Our greatest fear is to lose a loved one to death. How do we overcome this attachment to another and let go the fear that someday they will no longer be in our lives?

One of the steps a person goes through in a grieving process is blame. This is either directed towards the person leaving them or they blame them self for not being able to do something. Only with a strong, stable base, developed through the lower chakras, are we able to be strong and face such adversity.

The tragedy of losing one's own son or daughter definitely tops the list of challenging this strength. It would be difficult for any human being to deny the emotion of fretting or fearing the loss of one's own son or daughter, let alone be able to bear the grief of that loss and heal the pain that comes with it. We are human beings—this emotion is primal. However, the capacity to sense our attachment for that loved one and move forward requires a developed consciousness. A person who can recognize suffering is a part of life has a better chance of accepting the loss.

### Experiencing Heartache and Loss

A heartbreak or heart-opening of such measure can only be identified through actually experiencing that loss. The only way to heal that loss is through surrendering. If we lose a friend, loved one or family member, it changes us. This could also come about through illness or any other tragic event that brings us close to death. We change our perspective on life. We change our priorities by having more family time and connecting more frequently with friends who are supportive. Moreover, we may realize material possessions have no value compared to important people in our lives.

My husband and I experienced a deep loss when we lost his son, Nikos, who was only twenty years old. Being witness to my husband's grief was extremely heartbreaking. I remember the night we heard this dreadful news, I think my body went into shock. As the days and months passed, I questioned how we would ever get through this. My husband appeared incredibly strong despite this tragic circumstance but there were plenty of days he wasn't able to cope with the tragedy and I witnessed a heartbreak that, to me, was beyond measure.

Not long ago, I got a glimpse of that deeper loss with my own son. He was a teenager, living his life like a typical adolescent. On more than one occasion, he found himself in trouble. The circumstance and seriousness of that caused him to lose his self-esteem. In his own words, he told me he didn't want to live anymore and I was shocked to hear this. I didn't know what to say but somehow I pulled it together. The words that came to me were from a higher source. I told him that I loved him very much and that I was glad he had the courage to share those feelings with me. That was all I could think of and I prayed for him to be strong and to have faith.

A part of me wanted to blame myself for his sense of despair but I also knew it was his life and a part of his learning experience. He had certain things to heal and to resolve and I was there to help him. Fortunately, I had already worked through my own feelings of despair and I was able to forgive myself.

To some people, suicide appears narcissistic and is considered to be an action of feeling sorry for oneself. I am here to tell you that this emotion lies much deeper than that. Unless you have been there, it is difficult to understand what goes through a person's mind. To overcome the feeling of hopelessness, a person will need to surrender. This person will also want to understand self-forgiveness. This is a big part of the heart chakra center.

If we are unable to forgive our self or our loved ones that have caused us pain, we will remain a victim and continue to suffer. In this case, our hearts remain broken or closed off. If we remain unable to forgive, we will refuse to ever let anyone get close to us because we unconsciously fear losing them. It seems easier to let someone control our emotions rather than simply allowing forgiveness for them or for our own self. Thus, this emotion blocks our awareness of love's presence.

To not forgive is akin to drinking a little poison each day and unconsciously expecting the other person to die. Alternatively, if we can forgive through our heart it cleanses our mental field. It clears our misconceptions and allows us the capacity to resonate with a higher vibration. Thus, we move forward into the higher chakras, connecting on a deeper level with the throat, brow and crown energy.

## Forgiveness Goes a Long Way

To pose this capacity of forgiveness from a different angle, I recently observed myself in a jealous circumstance that resulted in me having to take a hard look at forgiving myself. I recently observed my husband and a single woman becoming quite friendly and connected with each other. Whenever I saw them together, they were engaged in each other's attention. At one point, I seriously wondered if they were having an affair. I noticed myself becoming very skeptical and I confided in some friends. From my description of details, they too became suspicious. However, by my willingness to express my vulnerability and share my emotions with others, it helped me look at this situation from an objective standpoint.

I noticed my emotional attachment to this jealousy and questioned why I would feel this way. An easy answer popped in my head. I realized that I had once been the perpetrator. In this circumstance, I felt like the victim but then I remembered Manjushri and the role of being both the victim and the seducer. Owning my actions in this realization left me dumbfounded for several days. I felt very ashamed of my past behavior. I had to remain in this humbling place of regret and shame and allow for some self-forgiveness. This was not easy.

Any experience of deep forgiveness, for oneself or for another, does not come without a process of letting go. This involves telling the ego to step back and take a break while the true self opens to the healing process and finds gratitude in the circumstance that caused him or her pain.

The ability to let go, or the bliss that comes from any kind of forgiveness, is indescribable. The ability to reach the depth of this emotion often requires a trusted, spiritual practice. Forgiveness and trust go hand in hand. Connecting to a Divine source through prayer or through a deep, meditative state increases one's chance of trusting and the ability to forgive. To experience this power of letting go often requires surrendering to Divine guidance. I experienced this deep sense of surrender in a Holotropic session. This experience relates more to a blissful state of love than a letting go, but I had to let go before I was able to reach the bliss.

## Trust

Often in the Holotropic Breathwork trainings, fellow students are apprenticing. In the beginning of my training, many of the student apprentices were strangers to me. I didn't know who they were and therefore I didn't automatically trust them. I already had a lifelong history of not trusting people. This could be a result of what happened to me in my youth but it could also be that it is common in our society. People want to know someone well before they can trust them.

In one of my Holotropic sessions, I heard a voice inside telling me to trust in all things and to know that I was never alone. Just then, I opened my eyes for one second and saw an apprentice standing near me. She looked at me but I closed my eyes quickly. Her instinct led her to lie down beside me.

Prior to her doing that, I felt very alone. I was suspicious and skeptical that anyone could ever be there for me. When she naturally came over and hugged me, it felt like she was an angel of God. I then heard the voice of Jesus telling me "You are never alone and you have never been alone. I am by your side and you are always protected." I remember crying tears of joy for that message in my head. The experience was bittersweet and I will never forget those words. In fact, I make it a continuing practice to honor my relationship with Jesus' beloved presence. The love I feel for Him makes it easier for me to forgive. His presence in my life helps me remain in a place of trust and stay open to all beings. However, I am human and I am subject to the layers and layers of my heart chakra too. Life evolves and we are continually exposed to society and other people's energy. Therefore, it is a continuous process or in the Sufi philosophy, "a continuous polishing."

On another occasion, I had a Holotropic session that involved both Jesus and Inanna. The experience was very deep but I still remember the details. Mainly, I remember a moment of everlasting union and bliss. I saw Jesus and Inanna as two spirits holding hands. It was like they were connected energetically. When I think of the sacred marriage ritual, I think of this image when I experienced Inanna and Jesus united in Divine love. It was the most beautiful thing I ever experienced in all of my altered states of consciousness. It left me breathless and speechless. I found it difficult to share the profundity of that session with the sharing group.

That session left me with such a profound and blissful peace that I didn't want anyone to make fun of it. It felt truly sacred to me so I titled the experience, *The Sacred Union.* The development of my research with Inanna led me to a stronger understanding of this Holotropic session and I realized that my psyche was actually giving me an indicator for the future. In fact, once my assignment of this book is complete, I will begin to explore this dynamic duo in more depth. It will be the basis for my next book and I will be thrilled to finally express more of this powerful session.

### The Polishing

Last but not least, I want to share the bliss my husband and I experienced when we first met. It reminds me of Inanna and Dumuzi. We fell so hard and fast in love and we were both elated to have found each other. He and I were perfect together; it was like we were made for each other. We seemed instantly conjoined. We could barely stand to be apart yet we lived a couple hours distance. When we were together we completely connected and relished in the sweetness of each other's presence and the joy that all love brings. We experienced the bliss of the holy gardens. Nine months later we had an extravagant wedding ceremony which was well attended by all our friends. We were in love; therefore, we lived in a state of heavenly bliss.

In any new relationship, this heavenly bliss doesn't usually last. In an effort to not discourage anyone from falling in love, I want to add that a relationship could also spiral back around to becoming a more integrated heavenly gratification. The reality is we often have to undergo a process of disappointment before this state of balance can take place.

When we fall in love, we feel vulnerable and exposed. At some point, it is likely the other person will hurt us because we have this idealistic perception that they are perfect. We must undergo a transformation, or a "learning curve" in order to love another unconditionally and to trust him or her completely. Moreover, most relationships usually go through a cycle of ups and downs before they completely connect and find balance.

My husband and I were not even married six months before the sudden tragedy of losing his son took us out of our blissful state. It was not easy to stay clear and conscious. We were so out of sync that it took a lot of inner work for us to remain married. Yet we are both grateful for the mirror and the continuous polishing. We know the importance of struggle on a deep level and we have been able to stay together despite the distress.

In the next chapter, we get a glimpse of how important inner work is and what Inanna does to overcome it. Inanna steps up to the plate without question and takes a journey to the inner depths—the underworld. She is willing to embrace the unseen parts of herself in order to grow and continue onward and upward, thus reaching her highest potential.

# Chapter Six-
## Journey to the Underworld

*Your vision will become clear only when you look into your heart.*
*Who looks outside, dreams. Who looks inside, awakens.*
*~ Carl Jung*


*From the Great Above she opened her ear to the Great Below*
*From the Great Above the Goddess opened her ear*
*From the Great Above Inanna opened her ear to the Great Below*
*My lady abandoned heaven and earth*
*to descend to the underworld*
*Inanna abandoned her office of holy priestess*
*to descend to the underworld*
*She abandoned her temple in Erech to descend to the underworld*
*She gathered the seven me and took them into her hands.*
*With her possessions, she prepared herself.*

*She placed the shugurra, the crown of the steppe, on her head.*
*She arranged the dark locks of hair across her forehead*
*She tied the small lapis beads around her neck,*
*Let the double strand of beads fall to her breast,*
*She wrapped the royal robe around her body.*
*She bound the breastplate around her chest*
*And slipped the gold ring over her wrist,*
*Inanna took the lapis measuring rod and line in her hand.*

*Inanna set out for the underworld.*
*Ninshubur, her faithful servant, went with her.*

*Inanna spoke to her, saying:*
*"Ninshubur, my constant support,*
*My sukkal who gives me wise advice,*
*My warrior who fights by my side,*
*I am descending to the underworld,*
*If I do not return, set up a lament for me by the ruins.*
*Beat the drum for me in the assembly places.*
*Circle the houses of the gods.*
*Go to Eridu, to the temple of Enki.*
*Father Enki, God of Wisdom, knows the food of life,*
*he knows the water of life;*
*He knows the secrets, surely he will not let me die."*

*Inanna continued on her way to the underworld*

*Then she stopped and said:*
*"Go now, Ninshubur, do not forget the words I have commanded."*

*When Inanna arrived at the outer gates of the underworld,*
*She knocked loudly.*
*She cried in a fierce voice:*
*"Open the door, gatekeeper! Open the door!"*
*The chief gatekeeper opened the door and asked:*
*"Who are you?"*

*Inanna said:*
*"I am Inanna, Queen of Heaven, on my way to the East."*
*The gatekeeper said:*
*"Why has your heart led you on the road from which no traveler returns?"*

*Inanna answered:*
*"Because...of my older sister, Ereshkigal.*
*Her husband, the bull of heaven, has died.*
*I have come to witness the funeral rites"*

*The gatekeeper consulted his queen, Ereshkigal.*
*He returned after strict instructions from her to bolt the seven gates.*
.
*Ereshkigal instructed:*
*"One by one, open each gate a crack. Let Inanna enter.*
*When she enters, remove her royal garments.*
*Let the holy priestess of heaven enter bowed low."*

*The gatekeeper returned to Inanna and allowed her to enter.*
*At the first gate, from her head the crown of the steppe,*
*the shugurra was removed.*

*Inanna asked:*
*"What is this?"*
*She was told:*
*"Quiet Inanna, the ways of the underworld are perfect,*
*They may not be questioned."*
*At the second gate, from her neck*
*the small lapis beads were removed*
*Inanna asked:*
*"What is this?"*
*Again she was told not to question the ways of the underworld.*
*At the third gate, from her breast*
*the double strand of beads were removed.*

*Inanna asked:*
*"What is this?"*
*At the fourth gate, from her chest*
*the breastplate was removed.*
*When she entered the fifth gate, from her wrist*
*the gold ring was removed.*
*At the sixth gate, the lapis measuring rod and line was removed.*
*At the seventh gate, from her body the royal robe was removed.*

*Naked and bowed low, Inanna entered the throne room.*
*Ereshkigal rose from her throne and*
*fastened the eye of death on Inanna.*
*Inanna was turned into a corpse and hung from a peg to rot.*

*When, after three days and three nights, Inanna did not return,*
*Ninshubur, her faithful servant,*
*Set up a lament for her by the ruins.*
*She beat the drum for her in the assembly places.*
*She circled the houses of the gods.*
*Alone, she set out for Eridu and the temple of Enki.*
*When she entered the God of Wisdom's holy shrine,*
*She cried out:*
>        *"O Father Enki, do not let your daughter*
>        *Be put to death in the underworld,*
>        *Do not let your bright silver*
>        *Be covered with the dust of the underworld*
>        *Do not let your precious lapis*
>        *Be broken into stone for the stoneworker*
>        *Do not let your fragrant boxwood*
>        *Be cut into wood for the woodworker*
>        *Do not let the holy priestess of heaven*
>        *Be put to death in the underworld.*

*From under his fingernail Father Enki brought forth dirt.*
*He fashioned the dirt into a kurgarra,*
*a creature neither male nor female.*
*From under the fingernail of his other hand be brought forth dirt.*
*He fashioned the dirt into a galatur,*
 *a creature neither male nor female.*
*He gave the food of life to the kurgarra.*
*He gave the water of life to the galatur.*
*Enki spoke to the kurgarra and galatur, saying:*
*"Go to the underworld,*
*Enter the door like flies.*
*Ereshkigal is moaning with the cries*

*of a woman about to give birth.*
*When she cries, 'Oh, oh, my inside!!*
*Cry also, 'oh, oh, my inside!!*
*When she cries, 'oh, oh, my outside!!*
*Cry also, 'oh, oh, my outside.*
*The queen will be pleased.*
*She will offer you a gift.*
*Ask her only for the corpse that hangs from the peg on the wall.*
*One of you will sprinkle the food of life on it.*
*The other will sprinkle the water of life.*
*Inanna will arise.*

*The kurgarra and the galatur heeded Enki's words.*
*They set out for the underworld.*
*Like flies, they slipped through he cracks of the gates.*
*Ereshkigal was moaning: Oh, oh, my inside!*
*They moaned: Oh, oh, your inside!*
*She sighed: ah!!, ahhh! My heart!*
*They sighed, ah, ah your heart.*
*She sighed my liver, they sighed your liver,*
*Ereshkigal stopped. She looked at them and asked:*
*"Who are you and what is it that you wish for?"*

*They answered: "We wish only for the corpse that hangs from the peg on the wall."*
*They were given the corpse and did as they were ordered..*

*Inanna arose....*

In the last chapter, we are filled with a state of blissful union based on Inanna and Dumuzi's sacred marriage ritual. The tone of this chapter changes significantly and we are faced with a decision to look within. Inanna appears restless and hears a call. When Inanna opens her ear to the Great Below she opens to understanding her inner wisdom. This call is answered by announcing her travels to visit the underworld and to witness her brother's funeral. She takes a risk to dive deep into her psyche. She doesn't question this inner call or the possibility of abandoning her status as Queen of Heaven and Earth.

Inanna is ready to know more about her whole self and this transformation is necessary to become a counselor and guide to the people of Erech. Inanna honors her intuition and her innate, primal knowing. She travels to the East which symbolizes purity, trust, vulnerability, truthfulness and rebirth.

## The Preparation

Inanna faces death and journeys to the Great Below in an effort to transform consciousness for all. In *The Hero with a Thousand Faces,* Joseph Campbell uses Inanna's descent to describe "the oldest recorded account of a passage through the gates of metamorphosis" (1949). Although Inanna's poems were written five thousand years ago, the principle of change and death are relevant at any time.

When Inanna prepares for her journey she gathers together personal garments of ornamentation and protection. Imagine preparing for a journey to a foreign land. More than likely you would pack some very important personal items. Inanna's prized personal garments represent an expression of who Inanna is and what she looks like. We are told that Inanna wears seven items. These personal items are about Inanna's expression of truth, vulnerability, devotion and her unique identification with death and rebirth.

She begins by placing the crown on her head. The crown is her *shugarra* which represents her status as Queen. Inanna then places the small lapis lazuli beads around her neck. Lapis is the color of a deep blue sky in spring and it is also the color of the throat chakra. It is a brilliant blue that emanates purity. Lapis lazuli augments psychic abilities while improving vitality.

When she straps on her breastplate, Inanna knows that body armor is of utmost importance. She is wise enough to know that shielding and protecting herself is an important part of her journey. Inanna does not risk putting herself in a vulnerable position. She transforms vulnerability into taking responsibility.

Inanna slips the gold ring over her wrist. Since ancient times a ring signifies continuity, strength, protection and a magical force (Tresidder, 2000). Inanna wears this symbolic circle to show how important it is that

101

the cycles of life continue. This is her mission and purpose, to establish the cycle of life, death and rebirth. The ring, even in current times, is a well-known symbol of eternity, union and completeness which represents eternal life (2000).

Inanna does not forget the lapis measuring rod and line. This is important to her because the rod is an ancient emblem of supernatural power. Symbolically, the rod (or wand) is associated with the potency of the tree, the phallus, the snake, and the hand or pointing finger. Inanna carries the measuring rod and line specifically in her hand. This is a direct statement that Inanna is a deity and carries with her supernatural powers that include immortality. When she covers herself with a royal robe she is identifying herself as a person of significant stature.

### Stripped of Her Nature

As Inanna travels through the gates of the underworld, she is stripped of her essential talisman. She is stripped of her wholeness. This mission is very important to Inanna and she trusts in her inner wisdom. In the first gate, Inanna must relinquish her crown, the marking of her status as a deity. She is startled, she says, "What is this?" She doesn't expect to have any of these items removed from her person. Yet she continues forward to seek wisdom and truth. At the second gate, Inanna's lapis beads are taken from her neck and at the third gate her double strand is taken from her breast. These areas resemble parts of Inanna's body having to do with the crown, throat and heart chakra.

The symbolic potential of these items indicate that her spiritual essence is being diminished. Based on the representation that chakras are connected to our spiritual energy, Inanna's journey to the underworld begins with the shutting down of the crown followed by the brow and throat chakra.

At the fourth gate, Inanna's breastplate is removed. She is left vulnerable and defenseless yet she carries on. Inanna's gold ring is removed at the fifth gate. Gold is a symbol of the sun which represents the solar plexus chakra. The solar plexus chakra looks like a gold ring of energy. Inanna's purpose and empowerment are taken away. By diminishing this part of her, she is susceptible to forgoing all of her efforts and her devotion to the cycle of life. The cycle of life, death and rebirth are not just essential to Inanna—they are the laws of the universe.

At the sixth gate, Inanna gives up her lapis measuring rod. As she lets go of this, her hand is parallel to the second chakra's location which has to do with sexuality. This yang energy—looking similar to the phallus symbol—means removing her creative manifestation as a deity. Finally, at the seventh gate, Inanna's robe is removed and she is left naked and bowed low. As she unknowingly prepares for death, Inanna is removed of all of her virtue.

Ereshkigal immediately fastens the eye of death on Inanna and she is turned into a corpse. Three days and three nights go by while Inanna hangs on a peg to rot. Unaware that she is experiencing her wounding, Inanna suffers extensively. She even risks all her earthly power to understand the knowledge of death and rebirth—life and stasis.

In *The Gospel of Thomas,* Elaine Pagels believes we all want to take a look within. She quotes the Gospel, "For whoever has not known himself, knows nothing; but whoever has known himself has simultaneously come to know the depth of all things" (1979). Of all the Gods and Goddesses, Inanna has the ability to journey between creation and dissolution and is given the ability to know the depth of all things (Meador, 2000).

### The Call for Help

After three days and three nights, Inanna's spiritual servant set out to find help. She is rejected twice but on the third try, Ninshubur pleads to Father Enki, God of Wisdom:

*Father Enki, do not let your daughter*
*be put to death in the underworld.*
*Do not let your bright silver*

*be covered in the dust of the underworld.*
*Do not let your precious lapis be broken into stone ........*
*Do not let your fragrant boxwood be cut into wood........*
*Do not let the holy priestess of heaven*
*be put to death in the underworld.*
*Wolkstein and Kramer, 1983*

Not only is Ninshubur persistent in her cries for help but she requests it with interesting imagery and symbols. Her requests convey an important message. She identifies the daughter of Enki as the feminine aspect of himself. She is letting him know that this part of him will remain dead unless he is willing to do something about it. The three elements: silver, the lapis stone and wood are pointed out. Silver represents the pure light of Inanna and its brightness reflects the light of the moon which relates to the feminine principle (Herder, 1993).

Stone is a universal symbol which connects heaven and earth (Herder, 1993). Inanna's holy servant is suggesting that the eternal, immutable, divine powers of stone or the permanence of earth, represented in the lapis stone, are being jeopardized. Permanence, strength and integrity are all suitable characteristics represented in the lapis lazuli stone (Tresidder, 2000). These distinct traits directly relate to Inanna's character.

Wood is one of the oldest and most important raw materials originally equated with matter. Wood is symbolically related to the complex of embracing or holding vital energy. Wood is related to the mother archetype because it carries, contains and protects life (Herder, 1978). Boxwood is the symbol of protection, the female womb and is a kind of tree.

Ninshubur is directing a message to Enki that without his assistance all these elements will disappear. Additionally, she is highlighting the importance of Inanna's status in the Sumerian pantheon. Inanna represents the permanence, strength and integrity of mankind and the connection between heaven and earth. Moreover, she represents the inner womb, the container and the protector of us all.

## Compassionate Ereshkigal?

Enki quickly responds and brings forth dirt from his fingernail to manifest sexless creatures that are neither female nor male—they are androgynous. Enki possesses the power to give these creatures the food and water of life and he does so with detailed instructions. When the androgynous (neither male nor female) creatures confront Ereshkigal, Inanna is already a corpse.

Ereshkigal is moaning and groaning like a woman about to give birth. This scene represents the importance of human expression. If we do not express our emotions—such as sorrow, pain or grief, we may never grow. If we stay within parameters that keep us out of reach with our feeling nature, how can we express our deepest emotions? As Ereshkigal moans and groans, she expresses pain. She is the victim now. Her pain is felt inside and out—in her heart and liver. She stops and looks at the sexless creatures that are echoing and acknowledging her cries. These creatures are gifted with empathy and are capable of mirroring the lonely queen's emotions. They are listening to her and she recognizes this.

In your own life, have you ever had the experience of another person being a witness to your deep emotional release? This can be a very powerful experience. It can awaken you to hearing your own voice. It can also represent being heard. Ereshkigal asks the sexless creatures, "Who are you?" She is softened by their affectionate manner and offers them a gift. She asks them, "What do you wish for?" The sexless creatures ask for the corpse and they are granted this wish. As they sprinkle the food of life and the water of life onto Inanna's body she is reborn. This action of sprinkling water and substance is comparable to a purification or baptism.

In *The Inner Reaches of Outer Space*, Joseph Campbell defines a purification or rebirth process. He explains that the transformation of character that is necessary to live in the light of a changed world is available in the throat chakra.

> The required method...is known as *the turning about of the energy,* which is to say.....an application of all the available malice and aggression of chakra three, not outward to the correction of the world, but inward, upon oneself; as in Jesus' thought: not removing the mote from one's brothers eye, but casting out the beam from one's own (1986).

Campbell describes this chakra's deity to be in demonic form. He describes this demon as a "manifestation of one's own impulse to aggression turned back on oneself, the vanquished shapes underfoot representing attachment to physical desires and the fear of physical death" (1986). Thus, providing an opportunity to see from the inside what we unconsciously manifest on the outside and then clearing oneself of the mechanical, automatic beliefs of fear and attachment.

### The Shaman

The story of Inanna's journey to the underworld can be related to the archetype of the shaman. The shaman is considered the holy man, the medium or the healer in a tribe. He or she holds a high status. The shaman is gifted with being able to travel from the earthly realms to the spiritual realms while undergoing a profound transformation. The shaman returns renewed, regenerated or reborn. Inanna's journey to the underworld can be viewed as a shamanic ritual.

Many cultures have used a natural psychedelic to inhibit an altered state of consciousness. Stan Grof worked with psychedelics for many years and discovered that this ritual-like process was comparable to a shamanic process. In Grof's research, the patient or participant went through a psychospiritual death and rebirth which resulted in a changed view of their life and of humanity—instilling a greater action toward service. This deep, meditative process can awaken an inner truth in someone that improves their perspective towards compassion and oneness. If enough people did some type of inner work, at whatever level works for them, this could produce a huge shift in the outer world for the benefit of humanity as a whole.

Holotropic Breathwork™ is comparable to the process of transformation in which one is able to go to the underworld and experience a psychospiritual death. When the person returns, they have the potential to change and transform their outlook on life. My experience of opening the box and witnessing Inanna emerge from the darkness is an example of the varying depths of Holotropic Breathwork or our inner consciousness.

Have you ever felt like you died to some part of yourself? Perhaps this part of you is no longer necessary. However, it involves consequence and surrender to Divine will. For most people, life changing circumstances are difficult because this involves learning a life lesson or experiencing a serious hardship such as illness, grief or financial loss. Surrendering to the experience takes a commitment towards responsibility which often results in living a life adhering to high moral principles. With this knowledge, one is able to better reflect an inner truth.

Integrity is an important life lesson. Ultimately, this helps one become a more whole person because it requires being honest with yourself. It requires having an objective viewpoint of your life. This is not an easy task and for some people it takes time or another person's perspective. For some people it takes journeying to the underworld and experiencing a transformative, shamanic journey to the spiritual realms.

### *Inanna's Replacement in the Underworld*

Inanna is about to leave the underworld but she is stopped and told:

*No one ascends from the underworld unmarked.*
*If Inanna wishes to return from the underworld,*
*She must provide someone in her place.*
*        Wolkstein and Kramer, 1983*

A part of Inanna must return. A passageway has been created from the Great Above—the conscious realms, to the Great Below—the unconscious, but it must remain open (1983). It would be too easy for Inanna to return from the underworld unmarked.

When she returns from the underworld, the first person she sees waiting for her is her beloved servant, Ninshubur. She is loyal to Inanna and does as Inanna requests. When Inanna sees her, she is still clothed in grief. Ninshubur throws herself at Inanna's feet and is willing to replace her but Inanna cries:

*No, Ninshubur is my constant support.*
*She gives me wise advice,*
*She is my warrior who fights by my side.*
*She does not forget my words!*
        *Wolkstein & Kramer, 1983*

Inanna is steadfast and clear that Ninshubur is the last person she would relinquish as her replacement in the underworld.    Inanna  returns  to  her  city  with  the underworld creatures standing by her side.

When she arrives at the gates of Erech, she sees Dumuzi under the apple tree. He is sitting on his magnificent throne, in his shining Kingly garments, when Inanna sees him. She is battered and bewildered but walks toward him. Dumuzi does not get up to greet her. In fact, he stays frozen in disbelief. Dumuzi was sure Inanna would not return. Inanna is heartbroken and reacts with impulse. She fastens the eye of death on her husband and the one whom she chose to be king of her city.

### Dumuzi's Turn

Dumuzi runs from the creatures of the underworld in fear of his own death.  He is not willing to experience what Inanna has faced and refuses to journey to the underworld. He fights back by claiming his mark as a human being—a mere mortal who has no powers without the presence of his beautiful Queen of Heaven and Earth (Wolkstein and Kramer, 1983. Dumuzi is faced with replacing her in the

108

underworld knowing he will not return unless Inanna specifically requests it.

Why does Dumuzi run? Why isn't he willing to surrender to Inanna's petition? Dumuzi is terrified of submitting to a place where he will become separated from all that brings him comfort. Dumuzi's sister, Geshtinanna, comes to his aid and becomes part of Divine order. She represents the holy grace and compassion that we often receive in times of distress and uncertainty. She finds a soft spot in Inanna and beckons her to free Dumuzi from the underworld for half the year. She will sacrifice and replace him for six months out of the year. This way, those who love Dumuzi, will not be completely in shock to hear the news of his sudden, unexpected death.

*You will go to the underworld half the year.*
*Your sister, since she has asked, will go the other half.*
*On the day you are called, that day you will be taken.*
*On the day Geshtinanna is called,*
*that day you will be set free.*
        Wolkstein and Kramer, 1983

Thus, Inanna places Dumuzi in the hands of the eternal. In that moment, he and Inanna are reconciled. Their relationship as king/queen, husband/wife, father/child, brother/sister represents the duality of male/female, positive/negative, spirit/matter that exists throughout the cosmos (Hart, 2010). Dumuzi's alternating six-month sojourn in the Great Below, along with six months of freedom, suggests nature's seasonal change from barrenness to abundance. In human life, this represents periods of inactivity—providing time for reflection and preparation—to periods of activity and expression.

Our modern society has not changed much in five thousand years. except we have a stronger tendency to feel satisfied by physical comforts which leaves us less interested in our spiritual needs. We have very little faith in our inner voice especially when it has to do with surrender. Surrender is important in our search for enlightenment but it can also bring on strife. It is true this process can be painful, but this pain will allow us to transform if we are open and ready to accept it. A worse case scenario is that we stumble in our suffering and never experience what the Divine has in store for us.

### The Throat Chakra

The Throat chakra links together the emotions and instincts of the active, lower chakras with the vision, reflection, knowledge and understanding of the brow and crown. The throat chakra is about expression. The communication can be either verbal or non-verbal. It is also related to the ear and has to do with listening or hearing. On a much deeper level, the throat chakra has to do with listening to our own voice. If we take the time to listen to our inner voice—or a call to higher wisdom—we will hear our soul guiding us.

Inanna hears a call to the underworld but this is considered an incomprehensible feat. Why would Inanna obey this call? In our modern world, it is becoming increasingly important for each of us to take a journey and explore the depths of our own inner psyche. This journey is often coined as "a wounding." Letting go through the process of "wounding" can open us to our mystical qualities.

Whatever our cross is to bear, the throat chakra is our place to heal the wounds through an outward expression. The healing that happens through expression manifests differently for all of us but it first requires acceptance and actually being present to the inner turmoil which can often feel like a death of the self. This death can then transform into an awakening or a symbolic rebirth. One way of healing these wounds can be done through creative expression. There are many ways to utilize creative expression. For example, writing, art, movement therapy or singing. It can also be done through moaning and groaning or embellishing vocal sounds to release blockages.

In Carolyn Myss' book, *Anatomy of the Spirit*, she considers the throat chakra a place where we continually question the challenge of God's will. She says the Divine can lead us primarily to learn about the nature of spirit

110

and of God (1996). She believes that the greatest act of will should be to live with simple principles: making no judgments, having no expectations and trusting in spiritual direction. She uses the well-known Serenity Prayer as a great example:

*God grant me the serenity*
*To accept the things I cannot change*
*The courage to change the things I can*
*And the wisdom to know the difference*

I wholeheartedly agree with this phrase and I always have the serenity prayer on my desk as a reminder.

When we listen and follow our inner guidance we do take a risk. This is usually not something of simplicity or ease. It is a task at hand that not only involves great danger but great possibilities as well. Ironically, it is always a blessing or a gift.

Within each of us is an inner healer or an internal healing mechanism. In some people, it is evident through a psychic gift. This is called being clairaudible and allows the person to hear internal messages. These messages can be from a person's spirit guide, higher Self or a loved one who has passed on. To truly channel internal messages, a person must have an open and loving heart as well as a developed brow and crown chakra.

Another aspect of channeling is called glossolalia. The gift of tongue is "a manifestation of the Holy Spirit in the sense that He gives this gift through sovereign grace to some in the Assembly and He works *in* them" (1 Cor. 12). This action manifests from being able to hear the language through one's ear and if one wishes, to speak it out loud. Most people have a hard time believing this because it is not a tangible reality. There is no one they can see talking to them; it is in fact, "all in their head".

Carl Jung describes this kind of experience as living in the ethereal realms. In his 1932 lecture, he says that only a select few have reached the energy of the throat chakra and entered the psychic gateways of the universe. This makes perfect sense considering the throat chakra's element is ether. Jung quotes:

111

With certainty we realize our psychic existence as the only reality through experience. [We can look] at the series of chakras as...the transmutation of crude matter to the subtle form of spirit. One would have to recognize that psychic facts have nothing to do with material ones. For instance, the anger you feel toward someone or something, how justified it may be, is not caused by external causes. It is a phenomenon onto itself. In other words, your worst enemy may be in yourself. If the psychic experience imposes itself on you, then you understand and you can make a concept out of it. The abstraction or projection...[results] from experience (1932).

Moreover, Jung is stating that psychic facts are a reality in the throat chakra. The Sanskrit name for the throat chakra is Visuddha which means purity, essence or truth.

The truth of the throat chakra is much more than stating facts. It has integrity, power and depth. Some people easily create stories about others based on their own internal process. The throat chakra is identified with our vocal chords and our outward communication. When we begin to get familiar with this chakra's depth and sincerity we recognize that derogatory gossiping is an unconscious result of low self-esteem. It manifests out of one's unconscious suffering and pain.

Another scenario to consider is whether a person is living in an environment where he or she has full expression. To heal this "silent child" archetype one must undergo a vulnerable process of clearing up old wounds in order to speak out about his or her true feelings (Wauters, 1997). This person may feel a deep need to be heard. The best outcome for healing the silent child archetype is to share in a compassionate, supportive group. This is the principle of bearing witness which can be beneficial for everyone. This concept of *being* a witness for another and *bearing* witness are equally compatible means for healing.

Full Expression

In the Holotropic Breathwork™, often times people are expressing deep emotional wounds. The approach for this work allows the breather to feel whatever emotions and expressions come up. An extremely profound healing can take place if the container to hold this space is safe and supportive. If not, a person can suffer even more. It is important for the facilitators of this work to be compassionate and non-judgmental while trusting that the breather's inner healer is guiding their work. This requires a level of maturity and integrity that is compatible with the throat chakra.

I personally have had several Breathwork sessions where I used my voice to express emotions such as anger, agony and despair. A couple of months after I did the Breathwork in Richmond, VA, I went to a week long training workshop. During that week, I was able to get in touch with my anger and sadness about not getting custody of my son. By expressing this in a safe and controlled environment, I was able to work through these emotions and recognize them in my daily life. I was able to get in touch with my feelings and understand how emotions were controlling my life.

*Journey into the Darkness*

Over time these Holotropic experiences brought me more in touch with my emotions. As I grew older, I had another force to contend with. A common occurrence that almost every woman can relate to is PMS. When I am in the middle of my cycle and experiencing PMS, I have an insatiable desire to crawl into a cave. This relates to the term I used in an earlier chapter called the "moon hut." I feel like a part of me is dying and from a physiological standpoint, it actually is. Another egg has bit the dust. Emotionally, it feels like some wretched inner turmoil that has me trapped and tied in knots.

In Chapter Two, I explained that this change in a woman's hormones can be identified with the "wild Lilith" archetype. When this change takes over, I immediately try to fight it. However, I am learning to honor it more and use it as a catalyst for my own process of transformation. Let me be clear, it doesn't always work out smoothly but with good intention, good does come out of it. If I learn to surrender to these spiking hormones and listen to my inner voice without blurting out obscenities, I feel like I have made some progress.

Most women would rather be at home or in nature when they are experiencing premenstrual tension. I have asked other women and they simply nod their head in agreement. They know words are not necessary. We try to explain it to men but they never fully get the gist of it. Instead we are labeled hysterical or worse yet, "a bitch." In a way there is some truth to it because it represents the archetypal "wild woman" or the unconscious, underworld Ereshkigal.

The best thing for me is not to go into a cave, it is better if I immerse in nature. I love to be in nature when I am feeling vulnerable and exposed. Nature rejuvenates my love for spirit. Experiencing the smell of the flowers, plants and trees, listening to the birds chirping and various sounds of animals—all of this lights me up. My senses are heightened and these experiences in nature represent exactly what I need during my "moon hut" time of the month.

In Chapter Four, I introduced Robert Johnson and his theory that we have lost our feeling nature for bigger, better and more. In *The Handless Maiden,* Johnson states that the only way we will heal our lost inner feminine nature is to find solitude in the forest. He shares that we do not recognize the curative value of nature.

If we immerse in nature and connect with those parts of our self that welcome solitude, we can regenerate and feel renewed. According to Johnson, this is what it will take in order for us to heal the wounds of our inner psyche. On the other hand, if we continue to behave as victims and react to betrayal or abuse, we will continue to believe that we are not valued and unconsciously project our hurt on others.

Carl Jung says there are stages one goes through to transform from living a subjective experience to an objective one (1932). He says we must recognize that we are perhaps identical with our own worst enemy. Rather, our worst enemy is within ourselves. Each one of us can look in the mirror when we are projecting or blaming another for our pain. Johnson is suggesting that we all take a look within and spend some time reflecting on our own perceptions to understand why we react certain ways. With this inner knowledge, we may finally realize the truth that sets us free.

Stories and myths of ancient times have been told for thousands of years because there is a message in it for us. It is healing for any person to connect with stories because it helps us to relate to our own current circumstances. If we want to connect with our inner feminine nature, this story gives us a way to understand the importance of our feelings and emotions.

Many stories told throughout the ages deal with struggle and strife because they are a part of being human. In the world of modern medicine, no one has to feel hopeless or exposed to uncontrollable emotions. Generally speaking, many people prefer to completely avoid any pain or emotions. Our pharmaceutical industry is evidence of that. In the last ten years, there has been a significant rise of prescribed pharmaceuticals for pain and emotional imbalances such as depression and anxiety.

## What Are We Running From?

There are legitimate circumstances where prescription medicine is necessary. However, instead of taking a look within and dealing with the core issue of pain or emotional imbalance, many people take a pill so they don't have to feel anything. Additionally, the current statistics among teenagers show that the abuse of "street" drugs is on the decline and pharmaceutical drugs, such as oxycotin, are on the rise. This is a serious problem for our country because our future leaders are exposed to medication that takes away their feeling sense.

In general, pharmaceutical drugs only mask the problem; they are not intended to heal the body. We have natural healing medicine available to us and we have alternative, all-natural techniques for self-help. There is a vast amount of natural modalities that could benefit someone in working through a situation rather than control or cover up their emotions. Emotions and illness are indicators that our body, mind and spirit are out of balance.

Chinese Medicine is an alternative medicine that helps one identify with the unseen, internal energy. It is based on the energetic meridians of the body. Everyone has these meridians just like everyone has chakra energy. Both are important systems for understanding the *qi,* the energy that flows through our body. Chinese Medicine is an ancient, holistic approach to healing. This philosophy treats the body as a whole rather than in separate parts. Knowing the body from inside out aligns with a need for self-knowledge.

America's health care system could allow people to become more educated about their health by offering holistic options. In many cases, people cannot afford to pay for alternative medicine and are subject to what insurance companies and government subsidized support systems will cover. This minimizes the amount of people that can benefit from other culture's healing philosophies let alone nutritional advice.

Chinese Medicine, Homeopathic or Ayurvedic medicine emphasize wellness through a good diet, physical exercise and drinking plenty of water. When treating symptoms, Eastern medicines focus on restoring balance. Western medicine focuses on reducing symptoms but fails to recognize the importance of prevention. Western medicine is masculine, always reacting, whereas Eastern Medicine is feminine, preventing illness and striving towards harmony.

These two medicines can be integrated and used together for the best outcome of patients. Western medicine is necessary and has great value in the world by helping people in emergency situations and with surgery. The value of pharmaceutical medicine is controversial. Eastern medicine is equally important because its focus is on prevention and relieving a person's symptoms while restoring a person's health. Together they can be the medicine of the future.

If you take a look at Appendix A, which explains the basis of Holotropic Breathwork™, you will see that in ancient times and in many modern practices, it is perfectly acceptable to be in touch with our human emotions. Our ancestors did not have modern medicine available to them. They used natural methods and supported each other to work through imbalances. In many circumstances, our ancestors as well as our beloved Saints, were strong and courageous. They were willing to face the dark depths of suffering that many of us have chosen to avoid today.

## A Psychospiritual Death

Jesus is a great example of the human capacity to withstand suffering and pain. What did Jesus do? He faced strife head on knowing death was his only outcome. He was willing to do whatever it takes to fulfill the prophecy of what he heard his Father tell him. Thus, after three days he was reborn and transformed.

The story of Siddhartha has a similar message. His story tells us that he was called to leave the comfort and serenity of his palace. He surrendered to this inner call to leave the palace so he could experience human suffering. This led him to a psychospiritual death and rebirth. Thus, he embraced the suffering of humanity as a gift and became Buddha—the Enlightened One.

More often than not, the catalyst for one's inner healing comes from surrendering to the experience. As I mentioned before, this event could look like a severe illness, the loss of a loved one or an addict hitting bottom. Until we experience this wounding in our life, we will not be able to connect with our body or are emotions, and stay present. Many opportunities will arise over one's lifetime to answer the call or hear the voice of wisdom but most

117

people won't answer it until mid-life. We have labeled this a "mid-life crisis." However, this is not an absolute guarantee. We can only "awaken" when we are ready to take a look within. That can only happen when the time is right. Hopefully, we will be subject to an "awakening" sooner rather than later.

I underwent a series of circumstances when I turned forty—a ripe time for transformation. I moved, got married, and opened a wellness clinic. At the same time, I was challenged with some serious family issues. This was followed by a devastating, tragic loss. When Nikos, my stepson, died by suicide, my earlier suicidal tendencies resurfaced and became more intense. As time progressed, I found myself depressed and disconnected with the outer world. I completely forgot about my spiritual connection or praying to God for help. I felt alone and it seemed like there was no one to turn to for support. For several months, I experienced a "dark night of the soul."

At the bitter depths of my despair, I suddenly realized that through this process I was dying, but it was the result of a psychospiritual death. Because of my education and experience in Transpersonal Psychology, I was able to sit with these feelings. I was not interested in taking pharmaceuticals to numb the pain. I knew that with faith and trust everything would be alright. I also knew I needed help and reached out to my counselor.

My confidant and close friend, Jane, helped me through this situation. She helped me with understanding my feelings, added some awareness to the scenario but mostly, she guided me with her own intuition and compassion. Because I confided in Jane, knowing her background as a Licensed Mental Health Counselor and Certified Holotropic Breathwork Practitioner, I was given the opportunity to rebirth and transform.

When I realized that the only way I was going to survive was to change my perspective, I opened my heart. It was important that I was conscious through this process. To evolve, I had to become aware of my whole Self and it was essential I stay connected with my spiritual nature. In this place of adversity, I had to recognize that "this too shall pass." I did the best I could. Most

118

important, I had to realize that in each moment I had everything I needed to survive.

Since then, I have learned to "let go" and surrender to a higher wisdom. This process helped me have a better appreciation for my family and friends. I started volunteering and doing service projects in my community. I developed a deeper understanding that there is more to life than my individual self.

## The Way Through

One thing I began to understand through my "dark night of the soul" was the importance of going through it. I had to allow it and embrace it, instead of resisting it. The Holotropic experiences helped me understand this and they were my basis for strength in undergoing difficult times. This is where I learned the importance of growth and transformation.

The transpersonal experiences I had helped me recognize there is more to our bodies and our skin-encapsulated ego. Without these experiences, I may never have survived that recent dipping down and journey into the dark depths of my soul, or worse yet, I might still be stuck in unconscious patterns.

While I was writing my Masters Thesis, I decided to experience psychedelics in a safe setting. This was the only time I used a chemical substance to inhibit an altered state of consciousness. The opportunity came up while I was reading Grof's research and studies about LSD. I did this with the intention of diving deep into my psyche. I considered it a spiritual or shamanic ritual with the intention to die to my ego. I wanted to understand all things and be reborn. However, using psychedelics to enter an altered state felt more like the process was happening to me instead of allowing the process to happen naturally. It definitely happened and it wasn't the least bit comfortable. Within this lengthy process, I had a unique experience of leaving my physical body for several hours. When it was complete, I felt a sense of coming home to my spiritual Self. This experience felt like pure peace and a deep knowing of my inner essence. Not only did I undergo

119

a death of my "old" self, I sensed a strong spiritual connection filled with love and compassion for others. The whole process felt like a deep and profound purification.

Throughout my Holotropic Breathwork training, I had a multitude of experiences that ranged from physical sensations to floating in the cosmic realms. Another theme that remained consistent in my sessions was connecting with an eagle. In one session, the eagle gave me the opportunity to rise above and asked me to climb on top of him for a ride. I hesitated for a second but then hopped on and we slowly flew up the mountain to a tribe. I felt safe there, I connected and I was willing to rise up further. I knew I had the capability to rise above but the eagle was there to nudge me along. This session was significant for my development and represented movement up into my visionary aspect or brow chakra.

In the next chapter, I will share a poem titled, *The Cosmic Eye*. I had a conversation with this cosmic eye in a Holotropic session. It had an undeniable matter-of-fact tone regarding the acceptance of all things. I was told the world we live in is filled with paradox and should be accepted for what it is. This voice told me that we will only continue to self-destruct our human nature and our environment unless we choose to honor the opposites as one. Through this transpersonal experience, it became clear to me that we are fooling ourselves when we only honor the light and therefore, dismiss our shadow nature.

The following two chapters start with Sumerian temple hymns that were translated by Samuel Noah Kramer. Inanna's legacy continued for several hundred years as a Goddess who watches over her people and was worshipped. She resembles the visionary and the all-knowing, all-embracing Divine presence. She is Venus, the radiant star in the sky, and cycles between being seen in the morning and in the evening.

# Chapter Seven –
## The Morning and Evening Star

*Honored Counselor, Ornament of Heaven, Joy of An!*
*When sweet sleep has ended in the bedchamber,*
*You appear like bright daylight.*
*When all the lands and the people of Sumer assemble,*
*Those sleeping on the roofs and those sleeping near the walls,*
*When they sing your praises and bring their concerns to you,*
*You study their words.*
*You look with kindly eyes on the straightforward*
*And give that one your blessing,*
*You render a cruel judgment against the evildoer*
*And destroy the wicked.*

*At the end of the day, the Radiant Star,*
*the Great Light that fills the sky,*
*The Lady of the Evening appears in the heavens*

*The people in all the lands lift their eyes to her*
*The men purify themselves, the women cleanse themselves.*
*The ox in his yoke lows to her.*
*The sheep stir up the dust in their fold.*
*All the living creatures of the steppe,*
*The lush gardens and orchards, the green reeds and trees,*
*The fish of the deep and the birds in the heavens,*
*My Lady makes them all hurry to their sleeping places.*
*The living creatures and the numerous people of Sumer*
*Kneel before My Lady.*

*The chosen ones prepare great platters for her.*
*The Lady refreshes herself in the land.*
*There is great joy in Sumer.*
*The young man makes love with his beloved.*
*My Lady looks in sweet wonder from heaven,*
*The people of Sumer parade before the holy Inanna.*
*Inanna, the morning and evening star, is radiant!*

The Lady of the Evening guides her people in the darkness
to a place of rest and purification. The people of Sumer
welcome this guidance and succumb to a place of inward

focus. They live in harmony even amidst the chaos. They honor the still point or the quiet, prayerful, and peaceful mind. They kneel before Inanna, the brilliant evening star, and show respect for her guidance. In gratitude, they prepare food and drink to worship her. The Sumerians are inspired and they connect with their beloved deity as she prepares them for their awakening. This kind of inspiration represents a joyful and inspiring relationship with the Divine.

### Venus is the Radiant Star

The radiant star that the Sumerians worshipped five thousand years ago is today the planet Venus. This magnificent star of the universe carries many meanings. For one, this planet is related to many feminine qualities and is specifically related to beauty. In *Symbols and Their Meanings*, Venus is the "aggressively bright emblem of warfare and life-energy as the morning star, and of sexual pleasure and fertility as the evening star" (Tresidder, 2000). Evidently, Inanna's iconic representation has only evolved to a change of her name but her paradoxical implications are still around today. In Indian Vedic astrology, Venus is known in Sanskrit as *Shukra*, meaning clear, pure or brightness and clearness.

In this Sumerian hymn, when the "ox lowers his yoke" the people lower their heads in honor and acknowledgment of the feminine nature and the cycle of death and rebirth. Purified, they can surrender and are reborn anew. They honor the cycle of life with great joy and are gifted with the ability to dismiss any trepidation.

In Joseph Campbell's book, *Thou Art That*, he explains that Eastern cultures are in touch with nature and they view the balance of opposing forces as part of a whole. The Hindu and Buddhist philosophies are ancient and they still practice the same rituals they did thousands of years ago. These rituals honor both Gods and Goddesses. These polytheistic cultures recognize the whole of nature and the influence of both light and dark energy.

122

Western cultures, on the other hand, focus on good against evil and view the two as separate. Campbell shares, "But by what right, this Eastern tradition asks, do we call these things evil when they are of the process of nature?" All things are part of the whole and consist of a set of opposites.

The joy expressed through creation carries the opposite side of suffering and destruction. Nature does not call one good or bad—it accepts and embraces all circumstances as a part of the whole. The Sumerians celebrate the cycle of life and stay connected to a Divine source to continue to strengthen their ability in understanding all things. They recognize that through this practice they can be close to Inanna and the transcendent force of life which permeates their entire existence. They continuously awaken, everyday, to their beloved and to their own inner truth and essence. Inanna affirms her relationship with the Sumerian people by manifesting in the morning and evening horizon—the place where heaven and earth meet.

### .The Balancing Horizon

When daylight ends and one looks out into the vast sea, the sky and the water appear united. For a few brief seconds everyday, in the morning and evening, the masculine and feminine are one. At twilight, the sun setting into the horizon is very calming. At dawn, there is a few seconds of silence before the sun appears. These few seconds happen every day and are filled with a deep, inner quality.

In the morning and evening, twice a day, Inanna is present when balance is restored. The morning star, opening to daylight, is considered yang in nature and implies masculine active energies. The Sumerian people gather in praise as Inanna oversees a structured, civilized order. The night offers a more feminine approach. The Sumerians prepare for their evening ritual which involves purification, quiet reflection and in some cases, lovemaking. As we can see from this stunning hymn, the people of Erech yearn to fulfill both their masculine and feminine aspects. They are satisfied with Inanna's influence and the ability to provide a stable, dependable cosmic order that guides and organizes life's activities.

The intention, intuition and structure of the Sumerian people are important to Inanna. This is how civilization developed over time—out of chaos emerges order. Inanna takes in all those who are willing to surrender their cares and concerns. In turn, she blesses those who kneel before her with sincerity and a straightforward focus. However, she does not hold back her aversion for those intending ill will on others. Discernment is required to keep order and it is within her power to implement. The Lady of the Morning settles the ruling principles on society so that the people of Sumer can direct their energies toward their days work (Wolkstein and Kramer, 1983).

Structure and balance help all of us make choices that encourage the best possible outcome for our life's purpose. Inanna represents balance when she journeys to the underworld and faces her own shadow. She is able to shed light on her deepest inner being and own it. We, too, can experience an inner journey which allows us to get in touch with our shadow consciousness. The willingness to be open and trust in our inner healer balances the psyche. With balance, we can surrender and trust in the Divine.

The temple poet writing the hymn acknowledges the masculine and feminine balance in Inanna. The morning star opens to daylight and to the logical, linear aspects of the brain. The evening star opens the mind to the inward, creative aspect. The true masculine/feminine integration, otherwise thought of as the yin/yang, includes a paradoxical understanding of nature. Nature does not hold the two as opposites but as one unified whole.

This is very similar to a quote written by Thomas Merton, he says, "There is in all visible things a hidden wholeness." Parker Palmer includes this in his book, *Let Your Life Speak,* and replies, "In the world of nature, a great truth is concealed in plain sight: diminishment and beauty, darkness and light, death and life are not opposites. They are held together in the paradox of hidden wholeness" (2000). Inanna represents this wholeness. She elegantly handles affairs, has clear boundaries, and shows righteous judgment for the better interest of the Sumerian people.

Those who genuinely live from the heart space, and acknowledge this balance that is hidden in nature, are granted the blessings of intuition and imagination. When it is time for the day to turn to night, when the masculine energy of our universe surrenders to the feminine, there is joy and union throughout the land.

### Having Expectations

Acknowledging the masculine and feminine balance within our consciousness gives more attention to our inner feminine nature. For example, we are expected to work and be responsible, productive citizens—a masculine aspect of consciousness. We are not, however, expected to meditate. This is a feminine aspect. I will be the first one to admit that meditation does not come easy. I always find far more important things to do. I have to remember that getting things done does not outweigh taking time to sit and relax or to meditate. When I have a project to complete, I find it very difficult to be quiet and meditate. Internal expectations, whether conscious or unconscious, are often created because society puts certain demands on us. In turn, we put these demands on ourselves.

Let's face it, in today's day and age we put a lot of weight on accomplishing goals. I often ask myself, how many things did I do today? I measure my good days by how much I've accomplished. However, if I want to be internally balanced, it is important for me to honor my down time. I need to take care of myself and to set a little time aside for nurturing my inner feminine. Then I can "lay down my yoke", my concerns and worries, and let my active mind rest. It is good for me to let all the busyness go and surrender to the Divine. If I can allow myself to be internally cleansed and purified, I will feel renewed and refreshed throughout the day. This is especially important for overall health and wellness.

Most people get up before dawn because they have to go to work. Can you imagine what the world would be like if we routinely got up before dawn to meditate or took some time to relish in the stillness of a new day? If all our time is spent on getting things done, we will never rest long enough to reflect on the intuitive or creative self. It is becoming increasingly important that each one of us explore and develop the serenity that results from an internal, meditative practice.

Evidently some people possess intuitive and visionary gifts without having a morning practice but imagine how their values would change if they did. I can't help but wonder what the corporate world would be like if people had time to meditate and connect with their inner visionary gifts. Undoubtedly, there would be more focus towards compassion and less competition among co-workers. However, this is not the point.

Some of the world's biggest business gurus already possess visionary gifts. Unfortunately, they are likely to be self-centered and ruthless business entrepreneurs. This is why it is common in the corporate world, that the higher up the ladder you climb, the tougher the competition is. This competitive, "cut-throat" nature is not for everyone and the reason many people don't make it to the top.

Rational thought and logic are governed by the left (masculine) side of the brain. Intuition is commonly related to the right or feminine side of the brain. So here we have intelligence vs. intuition. Sadly, our modern education programs emphasize the need to have scientific proof of things and discounts the more creative, intuitive or experiential learning.

Public schools are constantly cutting budgets. Art and Physical Education classes are the first to be cut. These are right-brain activities that inspire our children on a completely different level than math and science. It is common knowledge that children are creative and imaginative in early development. Why would we take that away and replace it with more logic? They will get plenty of that later in life.

## Balancing the Opposites

The idea is to balance both the masculine and feminine sides of the brain. If we consider how the Sumerians lived, we can see that they incorporated both sides of the spectrum. One should not outweigh the other.

There are plenty of people who live their life in a spiritual void but do not pay attention to the material world. These people have a great sense of connecting with their intuition but often times they don't have any business sense. Unless they are respected as a psychic, guru or mystic, they are thought of as flighty or unreliable.

Balancing the left and right parts of the brain is very important. When we are able to adapt to the changes of life and, at the same time, be grounded in ours bodies we can experience life as a flowing and profoundly mysterious event. Having a philosophy based on the value of personal experience and self-knowledge gives us a healthy and grounded way of responding to life.

Another concept to consider is when we restrict ourselves with preconceived expectations of how our life should be. We forget that we have this inner light or guidance within us. If we are constantly in a rush or in a "fight or flight" mode all day, we easily disconnect with our life trajectory.

A person who develops a balance between their masculine and feminine energy wakes up everyday satisfied with their accomplishments. They have let go of expectations and are not attached to the end result. They see life as a blessing and a gift no matter what is presented to them. This is not to say that they stop planning and achieving goals. They are simply satisfied. At this point in life development, having developed a healthy brow chakra, one should be able to surrender to whatever life brings. This outlook prepares us for the crown chakra, a place where we can truly live a life without expectation and let go of all attachments.

When we only live from the dictates of our left brain, the realm of logic and rational thinking, we miss the other half of life that is filled with joy. There is a whole spectrum of imagination, intuition and wisdom wanting to balance with our intellectual capacity. True balance requires acceptance of the unknown to match the fixed ideas and patterns of the intellectual life.

## The Sushumna

In Kundalini Yoga, there is a symbol of a staff with two snakes on either side called the caduceus. The staff is the central energy channel of the body and the Kundalini or serpent energy awakens at each chakra. The lateral channels represent the masculine and feminine—the yin/yang. The location where the staff, called the *sushumna,* and the two lateral channels, called the *ida* and *pingala,* come together (Davies, 2002). This is the brow chakra. The integration of the two channels is connected between the eyebrows because it is here where we are be able to perceive and project from a balanced viewpoint.

The healthy brow chakra allows us the ability to envision and see the possibilities not just for our self but for all people. The true visionaries are those who have chosen to live from their heart space and to serve humankind in general. They are coming from a completely different place than one who possesses greedy, selfish or narcissistic behaviors. The best leaders walk a fine line between the inspired world filled with intuition and the masculine, material world of action. A visionary is a medium between those two dimensions of higher thought and physical reality. He or she connects with a source of inspiration, yet is vitalized and manifests a specific vision.

For the Sumerian people, this vision streams through them because Inanna embraces the paradoxical realms. They are forced to awaken to their darkness and begin to shed light on those parts of the self that are no longer serving humanity or the community as a whole.

In Inanna's journey to the underworld, she can only see a few steps ahead, but she trusts in her intuition and perseveres. Inanna knows that in order for the people to prosper and live their highest potential, they must

128

recognize their imperfections. We can all learn something from uncertainties, challenges and personal shortcomings.

With a balanced and clear brow chakra, we are awake enough to make good choices. The choice at this level is to take the high road and learn from challenges in order to grow and become a visionary. We all have the ability to share our unique gifts with others. These gifts can be something like: developing mass communication, working with the ecosystem and/or environment, and helping the sick or homeless. Every human being has the right to sow seeds and manifest a vision towards their life purpose.

For some, this path includes spiritual progress—to develop and serve spiritually—with the hope of inspiring those around them. The Sumerian people are inspired by Inanna and her capacity to envision a civilized community. She also inspires them to connect with a higher source and relate to an archetype that walks a similar path.

It can be very helpful to connect with someone who has already experienced a "dark night of the soul." This person has lived to tell the story and come through the other side to support others on the path to wholeness. True visionaries can lift us out of the muck and mire and into the higher realms of human potential simply because they set a good example. Inanna possesses the qualities of the visionary and mystic; both correlating with the positive qualities of the brow chakra. Moreover, the best advice any spiritual teaching can offer us is the capacity to understand and develop our own inner knowing.

When you begin to trust your inner nature you will eventually become consistent with universal laws. These laws are ancient and have guided men and women for generations through the pathways of life. It is also important to realize our own value as a spiritual being. We must remember to trust in our intuition and follow our truth. It will help us find our inner wisdom. The answers to our questions exist inside our soul. Now is the time to access the depths of our inner experiences which have been culminating from lifetimes of learning. With this knowledge one can begin to develop an internal philosophy of life.

### The Brow Chakra

As we focus our awareness on the brow center, we open to the higher Self. This is the energy which connects us to the spiritual realms and aligns with an open crown chakra. If the brow chakra is open, we receive uplifting ideas which give us a sense of virtue and ethics. The higher Self, or our conscious awareness, serves as a guide or protector. This helps us deal with uncertainties in life.

A balanced brow center combines a clearly focused left brain, which computes and analyzes, and an open right brain which is where our intuitive, artistic and psychic gifts reside. Here we are taught discernment and wisdom. At the brow center, we focus on our inner and outer awareness at the same time. It is where we get our insight for well-being and happiness.

When we put intellect in the service of spirit, we find a way of developing inner wisdom. Discernment and other noble qualities are readily available to sustain us through life's crisis. So often people who primarily inhabit the left hemisphere of the brain and ignore the right hemisphere, do so because their feelings were ignored when they were children. Ignoring a child's needs and feelings is damaging because it forces him or her to live alone in the inner realms of his or her mind; never trusting their feelings or intuition.

In becoming conscious, one is able to detach from subjective perceptions and let go of expectations. Detachment does not mean ceasing to care. It means stilling one's fear-driven voices. Carolyn Myss tells us, "One who has attained an inner posture of detachment has a sense of self so complete that external forces have no authority within his or her consciousness" (1996). Such clarity of mind and self is the essence of wisdom. This inner wisdom is one of the Divine powers of the sixth chakra that fully prepares us to live in the present moment and experience an open crown chakra. We can finally let down our mask and reveal our authentic self.

130

The brow chakra has the same sound or energetic frequency as the star Venus or the ancient Inanna. If we were to listen to these tones and compare them they would be identical in promoting a great flow of love, energy and inner harmony. With a creative thought process, an open heart, pure intention and confidence, we can manifest our vision to be exactly what we hoped for and be able to live the life we dreamed.

### *Campbell's Words of Wisdom*

As an archetype, the brow chakra represents the visionary and the shaman. The shaman has been prevalent in indigenous cultures for thousands of years. Joseph Campbell often spoke about native cultures and their forms of rituals that were intended to allow one to enter into a trance or altered state of consciousness. Campbell's philosophy proved that the likeness of the Old World and New World could be evident in human psyche. He describes the New World iconography as the Navaho sand painting.

> In the Navaho sand painting the bounded area is equivalent to a temple, an Earthly Paradise, where all forms are to be experienced, not in terms of practical relationships, threatening or desirable, evil or good, but as the manifestations of powers supporting the visible world...The initiate actually enters physically into the painting, not simply as the person whose friends and neighbors have solicit[ed]...but equally as a mythic figure engaged in an archetypal adventure of which everyone present knows the design (1986).

Campbell adds that all the characters become "mythologized" so that the entire community is renewed and synchronized to the nature and beauty of their "spiritually instructive world." He compares this ceremony to the Kundalini staff or *sushumna* that was described earlier.

Campbell is a great example of a modern day mystic who was able to live in both the physical and spiritual realms. Campbell traveled the world and accumulated a wealth of knowledge that stemmed from his research and his actual experience in these rituals. He experienced the visionary realms through a variety of ethnic traditions and customs. He possessed the true visionary qualities necessary to spread the message that we are all capable of connecting to our own heroic journey. Lastly, he shares, "for the judgmental (didactic) eye, whether of negation or of participation, is governed by a very different order of shared suffering and love than the eye at the top of the pyramid, which is of God, the God that is without and within" (1986). I have personally connected to that "eye" on more than one occasion through my Holotropic Breathwork experiences. This relates to the brow chakra or what is often referred to as the "third eye."

Stan Grof tells us that many people have access to these transpersonal realms if they are willing. The key word here is willingness. We must first be willing to experience inner healing and grow in order to get the most benefit of a ritual.

The ritual process of Holotropic Breathwork™ is still only experienced by a select few. Yet these few are spread out and accessible in different countries which signify that humans are naturally drawn to this work. There is an inner call to connect to the spiritual realms and experience what exists beyond our skin-encapsulated ego. More and more people want to tap into the "third eye" chakra because it is a primal, innate part of humanity.

Some of my Holotropic experiences were so surreal that I had a hard time explaining them. It seemed there were no words—especially for the sessions representing the visionary or shaman. These experiences were extremely profound and detailed. In one particular session, I experienced a journey with an archetypal eagle. The eagle showed me many places and I wrote a poem immediately after the session that best describes my experience. This poem captures the essence of connecting to a higher Self and honoring a voice within.

## The Cosmic Eye

Clouds surround, pink-like
OK I'm here
Where am I going?
The cosmos once again
Swirling, open wide
Take me, take me
I'm ready to fly

Off to the tribes
Plenty of dancing
Feel the drums
My rhythm plants me
Into the universe
I'm off again
Spiral flying deeper
I finally see
Where it all comes from

The cosmic Eye
Tells me I have the vision
I alone can see
I have the power
Because I choose to believe

I want to know more
I ask about evil in this world
Yes, its here
This eye mocks me
Of course you know it's in the world
Where would we be
Without paradox of divinity
The balance of yin-yang
The devil & Lord God
Laughing, he says "This you know"

No more questions for me
Just take me to where I need to be
The universe is so diverse
Is wonderful to actually see

Then why is there plague & tragedy?
Is evil involved in all of this
It seems more like evolution
Or transformation
Suffering to realize good
Happiness abounds in their souls
As they sing & dance
while doing their chores

The devil thinks he's got me
And so I go deeper south
He greets me there
Letting me know he's in control
'Fuck You' I say a thousand times
You will never control my mind
I shun him away as he laughs out loud
"I will always be around"
Ignoring his response, I head back

Back to the cosmic eye
What next, where next
At once I am to see
The destruction of the earth filled green
Not so good
How can it stop?
I am alone
I must act fast
The shuttle starts and vibrates with glow
Here I Am
And now off I go

Running, running as fast as can be
All alone I can't believe
How can I tell them
They must stop and realize
It's US this time

Suddenly the eagle reappears
Willing to help spread the word
He takes off around the world
To spread the news
We are killing Mother Earth
I thank him so for his help
For I could not do it alone
He says, 'as you wish is my command,
I am happy to serve you, my 'high priestess'

Huh?..I think, but there is no time
Non-stop in cosmic time...

This cosmic journey was by far the most bizarre. Ask anyone who has ventured deep into their psyche and they will agree—it is beyond words. If you have never heard of it or tried it, I encourage you to explore this work sometime. This practice is in a league of its own because it can be so existential. Therefore, it requires a trained facilitator who understands the intensity of the spiritual realms. Also, this work is not for everyone. There are some contraindications to health. It should always be guided by someone with training and experience.

Holotropic Breathwork is intended to cut through the ego. It is not intended as a practice to do at home or alone. At a minimum, a monthly practice will allow one to integrate the right-brained process of completely connecting with intuition while living in the world—chopping wood and carrying water. The person must stay committed to living in the material world through the left-brain and be open to connecting with nature or a spiritual practice. Over time the practice of Holotropic Breathwork will help a person become more in touch with the universe as a whole. By doing this, the person can stay associated to living his or her life as a spiritual being.

The ability to stay present and conscious of one's thoughts requires a connection with the breath or the *prana*, our life-force energy. It also requires a focused, meditative mind. The result of this practice is a constant connection and awareness of Divine presence. This connection and awareness is experienced through the crown chakra. Inanna is the epidemy of this energy. She is the thousand-pedaled lotus that continues to connect heaven with earth. In the next chapter, we will explore another hymn that venerated Inanna as Queen of Heaven and Earth. The Sumerians give us another glimpse of this legendary Goddess' connection and influence on human life.

# Chapter Eight –
# **The Lady of the Heavens**

*My Lady, the Amazement of the Land, the Lone Star,*
*The Brave One who appears first in the heavens—*
*All the lands fear her.*

*In the pure place of the steppe,*
*On the high roofs of the dwellings,*
*On the platforms of the city,*
*They make offerings to her*
*Piles of incense like sweet-smelling cedar,*
*Fine sheep, fat sheep long-haired sheep,*
*Butter, cheese, dates, fruits of all kinds.*

*They purify the earth for My Lady.*
*They celebrate her in song.*
*They fill the table of the land with the first fruits.*
*They pour dark beer for her.*
*They pour light beer for her.*
*Dark beer, emmer beer, emmer beer for my Lady*
*The saguh-vat and the lamsari-vat make a bubbling noise for her*
*They prepare gug-bread in date syrup for her*
*They pour wine and honey for her at sunrise.*
*The gods and the people of Sumer go to her with food and drink.*
*They feed Inanna in the pure clean place.*

*I say,"Hail!" to the Holy One who appears in the heavens!*
*I say,"Hail!" to the Holy Priestess of heaven*
*I say,"Hail!" to the Inanna, Great Lady of Heaven!*
*Holy torch! You fill the sky with light!*
*You brighten the day at dawn!*
*I say,"Hail!" to the Inanna, Great Lady of heaven!*

*Awesome Lady of the Annuna Gods! Crowned with great horns,*
*You fill the heavens and earth with light!*
*Mighty, majestic, and radiant*
*You shine brilliantly in the evening,*
*You brighten the day at dawn,*
*You stand in the heavens like the sun and the moon,*
*Your wonders are known both above and below,*
*To the greatness of the holy priestess of heaven,*
*To you, Inanna, we sing!*

The Sumerian people have a deep relationship with the Lady of the Heavens. They want to celebrate and please her with even the smallest details. Even the bubbling beer vat is part of the ritual to honor her. There are seven hymns that were sung to Inanna but this one clearly represents the stature of a deity that was worshiped throughout Mesopotamia for hundreds of years. She is a Goddess—she is the archetypal Venus. She eloquently represents a spiritual, crystal clear vessel in human form. Inanna appears to the people of her city as a spiritual icon.

### A Beacon of Light

Inanna fills the sky with light, she is a holy torch represented by Venus, the morning and evening star. The sky is universally associated with supernatural forces and symbolizes dominion, spiritual ascension and aspiration (Tresidder, 2000). It is a source of pure cosmic power. Inanna is mighty, majestic and radiant. She is a Goddess empowered through her grandfather, An, the Sky God and her father Enki, the God of Wisdom. Inanna's given title, Goddess of Love and War, represents the ebb and flow of the universe.

At one point or another, we all experience the flux of life. The mystery of human life connected with the mystery of nature is represented by a Divine creator. It is the feminine aspect of the Divine that produces fertility in the land. When Inanna and Dumuzi unite they shine with inner joy. Once a year this ritual was performed to emanate Inanna's pure, cosmic light as a manifestation on earth. Thus, the spirit of love descends and is continuously reborn on earth. Love is greater than death and yet death is also a part of Inanna's ever flowing cycle of life.

In this hymn to Inanna, it is obvious she is loved by her followers. They show gratitude by bringing her gifts that represent the prosperity of the land. They bring her cheese, butter, fruit and beer in appreciation of her love for them. All of these gifts meet their basic needs and the Sumerian people believe that this vast supply of food and

138

drink is attributed to Inanna's intention of filling the land with prosperity.

Thousands of years later, we still worship and praise a heavenly order for supplying us with the necessities of the human, material world. Many people still pray before a meal and thank God for the food on their plate.

Humans have the capacity to connect spiritually to a Divine consciousness on a day to day, moment by moment basis but few do. There are millions of people that pray at night or meditate throughout the day to show gratitude for the blessings in their life but there are just as many people who do not think about it at all.

Our western civilization and the state of our society today provide only a meager attempt to show gratitude to the Divine. Having a practice of attending church once a week or on holidays is not enough. We rarely take the time to experience the spiritual realm and commit to an internal, devotional practice on a daily basis. Prayerful meditation is a great example of a continuous integration between a material and spiritual existence.

The practice of assimilating masculine and feminine balance (at the brow chakra) should be practiced and integrated before we can truly digest the concept of oneness. For thousands of years we have been guided by mystics that practice this balance of energy. Today there are only a handful of mystics that possess the ability to live in a constant state of presence with the Divine. Most notable are his Holiness, the Dalai Lama and the late Mother Teresa. Their dedication and commitment to love for all beings was developed throughout their life and through years of devotion. They are representative of a human being who shows gratitude to the Divine for living in a material, human world.

Anyone who has developed a relationship with the Divine and shows gratitude for their life blessings will move toward understanding oneness and universal truth. In spirit, we are all on this path but we approach this wisdom through different forms and perspective.

### What is Universal Truth?

Universal truth encompasses an all-knowing, all-embracing universal wisdom with the capacity to transcend all things. Eventually, our goal is to accept this universal truth—this enlightenment, like a crowning of our spirituality (Tresidder. 2000).

Joseph Campbell describes enlightenment through the energy of the crown chakra. He sees this as "a transcendent light which is the energy of the living world" (1986). Campbell believes we must first culminate the vision of one's image of God before we can fully tap into this universal light. We must first develop our internal masculine/feminine balance before we can identify with the crown chakra. These two chakras go hand-in-hand. The crown chakra energy provides us the wisdom of universal compassion that is organically met through the integration and balance of our inner masculine and feminine energy.

Our crown chakra energy motivates us to seek an intimate connection with the Divine in everything we do (Myss, 1996). This is an individual experience directed toward releasing fears of the physical world and pursuing a relationship with the Divine. Developing the brow chakra paves the way to give us the capacity to perceive which path we choose to take. That path will either lead us to love or keep us in fear. The decisions we make will determine the vibrancy of our crown chakra. The sacred, universal truth of the crown chakra is to live in a perpetual state of Divine presence.

We can free ourselves from the constraints of our human brain and immerse in universal truth through transcendence and connection with a Divine source. All of this sounds well and good in writing but it is easier said than done. In fact, seeking a personal spiritual connection can make one feel vulnerable, tenuous or even a bit crazy. In *Anatomy of the Spirit*, Carolyn Myss tells us:

> Seeking a personal spiritual connection shakes us to our core. Our conscious or unconscious prayer to come to know the

140

Divine directly can sound like this: "I want you to move into my life directly and remove from my life any obstacle—be it a person, place, or occupation —that interferes with my ability to form an intimate union with you."

Not every person will have the strength and courage to actually surrender to Divine will. Yet every one of us was born with an inner essence that is capable of connecting with a Divine source.

If we choose the course of practicality and continue living in a space that manifests doubt and skepticism for our own growth, we will most likely continue to react through our ego. If we live this way, we have a tendency to succumb to our fixations and self-sabotage to prevent self-growth.

If we choose to live like a visionary, we will open our hearts and our energy will flow forward. We will allow the Divine to flow through us with a deep knowing that any outcome will be a gift. We know that all circumstances are an opportunity to grow. The more we appreciate challenges as growing pains, the faster we evolve towards keeping an open and healthy crown chakra.

When we can tap into universal truth, we manifest inner peace. This inner peace allows us to become enlightened and aware of inner essence. In the book, *Chakras and Their Archetypes*, Wauters describe the crown chakra. Wauters says, "True spiritual awakening is not an external manifestation, it is an act of releasing the mind of all negativity and letting the beauty and grace of the spirit shine" (1997). When we know in our hearts that the purpose of life is to manifest spirit and to experience presence, we are free to let go and be ourselves. This is when we fully accept our Self in that moment as whole and complete. We are perfect just as we are and we see and know that others are perfect too.

## The Crown Chakra

The crown chakra adds wisdom which helps understand the sense of oneness. When this chakra is open, a person is aware of the interconnected nature of all things in the world. The "Guru" archetype represents having mastery of the spiritual realm and is connected to the Divine while living in a human body (Wauters, 1997). Additionally, the guru represents a person who sees that we are all united in the world—or that we all come from one united source. This is the highest level any human can attain and is represented by the continuous flow of energy seen in the chakras. The awareness and energy of this person manifests as a brilliant crystal—pure and beautiful.

There is no separation between self and life at the crown. A person who views everyone interconnected and flowing with universal love has an open crown chakra. We all have the capacity to reach this level of consciousness through a practice of our choosing. Some of us will devote a practice to love, to peace, others to teaching or healing.

Many of us will be given opportunities to be in service for others which will in turn feed our souls. If we choose to transform our lives to serving a higher vibration, one that resonates through sound and light, we will answer the call. With this intention and a strong connection to a beloved source, our light will emanate the message of love.

The crown chakra is where we have the ability to connect with the transcendent dimensions of life. This energy generates devotion, prophetic thoughts and mystical connections. It is like the Kundalini energy that pours upward and out of the crown chakra only to return through the root and continue in a cyclic flow of energy. When this happens, a fountain of glorious color, energy and light opens all the chakras and thereby allows human beings to self-actualize through gratitude and a partnership with their beloved. This is the pure light that is so appealing. When one has experienced all of the stages of life and continues to clear the chakra energy, this light gets stronger and brighter.

The world becomes a shimmering place when the crown chakra is open because the lens has been cleared and the light shines through. This light manifests all the capacities of humankind, including the shadow parts. These shadows are within the shining light because they are a part of the whole that is loved and accepted equally.

To experience the crown chakra energy means we accept responsibility for every aspect of our life. We have the ability to make choices that determine whether or not we want to be free or stay trapped in our ego fixations, keeping us from attaining enlightenment. At the crown chakra, we are able to transform and be a good example representing a clear, conscious person.

Recognizing that suffering is a part of life helps us view the universe as a continuous flow of energy that will continue to evolve. Each moment passes as an eternal cycle of suffering, surrender and bliss. If we are grounded in our bodies, we are able to accept the ever changing world that moves around us.

If we have an open and flowing crown chakra, we can truly experience living in the moment. Moreover, when we live with the awareness that every experience helps us develop a deeper spiritual connection, it is then we begin to live as the true visionary, the native shaman or the authentic guru. We can establish a strong sense of self once we accept that change is part of life. By loving our self and others, unconditionally, we move beyond our skin-encapsulated ego and enter into deeper interactions with others.

Inanna, the Goddess of Love and War, is committed to helping humans encompass this awareness. She dedicates her presence to represent quintessential compassion and light so that others may relate and follow her actions. She manifests as the light that exists in darkness to help us understand that the Divine is revealed in all aspects.

When working with the crown energy we are not only radiating love and peace within, we are sharing it with those around us. Inanna has an inspiring and charismatic truth about her that is influential to her followers. She radiates this guru-like energy that is all-knowing and all-embracing. In her presence, light and darkness are both accepted.

Originally heaven and earth existed as one united entity. According to this view, the sky or heaven represented half of the world and earth the other (Herder, 1993). In our modern world, it is more common to believe heaven and earth are two different places. They are two different sets of ideals in the mind—the ideal and its manifestation. Heaven is the realm of pure ideals and earth is what our thoughts manifest. We create our own ideals based on our perspective and outlook. The human body is the earthly manifestation of an inner heaven (Fillmore, 1931). In the crown chakra, we are given access to connecting with this inner heaven. Our state of mind is what determines how beautiful we are.

To experience inner divinity or "Christ consciousness" is to experience the blissful oneness that exists in the crown chakra. Charles and Myrtle Fillmore, the founders of Unity Church, initiated a new belief system that allows people to connect with their inner Divinity. In one of Charles Fillmore's writings, he compiled a *Metaphysical Bible Dictionary*. In this, he quotes, "Heaven is a state of consciousness in which the soul and the body are in harmony with Divine mind" (1931). This quote resonates with Jesus words when he spoke in parable, saying: "The Kingdom of Heaven is within you." Fillmore explains, "Applying some of the laws of mind as we know them, we find that Jesus was talking about universal truth and its expression." Fillmore believes Jesus was talking about our inner essence and the power of our inner conscious, not some distant realm.

### Connecting to a Divine Source

The image of someone's worship is a function of their own state of mind. This is inevitably a product of one's culture (Campbell, 1986). It matters not as much what the Divine and archetypal images are, as much as the recognition that they exist. In fact, Campbell explains a phrase used by the Hindu's. This is a tantric saying, *nadevo devam arcayes*, which means "by none but a god shall a god be

144

worshipped." Campbell says, "Catholic nuns do not have visions of the Buddha, nor do Buddhist nuns have visions of Christ." Moreover, the image of any God will be of a local ethnic idea which is culturally conditioned. It remains fixed whether it is of simple faith or a saintly vision. The image of the Divine is based on one's history and we naturally become attached to this appearance.

Through the ages, civilizations have evolved with manifestations and rituals of a Divine source. The common denominator in all cultures is that whomever they venerate, the image is powerful and illuminating. The names and faces of God may be different but there is no reason to believe one is greater than the other. For so long, we have been judging other culture's source of Divinity. It is time we open our minds and our hearts to accept our celestial inspiration and influence as one source.

Many people are finally recognizing this concept. In 1932, Carl Jung lectures that the expression and reflection of Divinity comes from our psyche and we are subject to what has been superimposed in our imagination. He suggests that we do not have to remain fixed in that belief. We can create whatever illusion serves us best. Ideally, this will enhance our connection with God. In other words, we can let go of fixed beliefs that keep our world separated by religious dogma. We do not have to create wars over religious beliefs. We were not created to convince others that one God is better than the other. We were created to recognize that we have free will and that we develop different images in our minds.

When we recognize that judgmental thoughts enter our mind, we are able to accept or not accept these thoughts. By awakening to our conscious thoughts, we awaken to our unconscious patterns. This process allows us to be congruent in how we think and who we show up to be. Instead of judging another or immediately dismissing one's personal beliefs, we can open our hearts and recognize that people are going to worship who they want.

We all have unconscious thoughts based on our beliefs, but the more aware we are the better chance we

145

have to be free. Through inner exploration, we have the ability to make conscious choices and create our reality how we want it to be. We can abide by societal and cultural beliefs or we can develop our own theory. Moreover, I think it is of utmost importance to know and develop our own truth.

The most prominent characteristic of the crown chakra is the connection to profound wisdom. Additionally, awareness and the right to aspire are also important. Inanna unmistakably possesses these qualities and is able to inspire those that desire the same qualities within themselves.

### *The God of Many Names*

The Creator, the One, the source of all energy and light is transforming and it will include many archetypal images for humans to draw from. There will always be God, but it will no longer be an image of an old man pointing his finger. The sinner era is over. Our future generations are not buying into guilt-driven religions anymore. Humans are naturally attracted to the presence of love and hope.

The generations ahead want to feel good and be empowered by their unique expression of self. This is exactly how it should be and this is Inanna's vision. She dreams of a Sumerian civilization that has integrity and is open and brave to life challenges. She allows people to express their creativity and their unique self. Inanna embraces all the aspects of the human race. If we have this awareness within and honor each others Divine qualities, we, too, may feel more whole and complete. We may recognize we are all a child of Mother Earth and Father Sky.

We originate from one united and Divine creator. Allah is an ancient name of God as well as the sky God, An, of ancient times. What is wrong with celebrating God's image in many shapes and forms? We have similar palettes but each masterpiece is colored by our inner view. We have a vision of creation based on our early perceptions that are beautiful in their radiant light. We have come from the same source but we have our own unique perception. This is our individuation; otherwise we would all be the same.

The Divine creator has expressed something beautiful in each of us. We are like snow flakes, created with our own unique, dynamic design. We have been blessed with a gift and an opportunity to share our uniqueness with each other and the beauty we feel inside.

Throughout world cultures we are aware of the many representations of God. Whether they are in human or cosmic form, they all display a powerful connection to Divine wisdom. If they are in human form, they possess a self-sacrificing commitment to humanity's evolution.

### Surrendering

Many people find it difficult to surrender to a higher wisdom—to experience the Divine within. For those that do, it is a private and personal experience. Very few will surrender to a mystical experience that portrays a figure of their own Divinity. One way I experienced this deep connection was in Holotropic session. Until now it has been difficult for me to share it with others because it is personal and private.

This was my second Holotropic Breathwork session at a workshop in 1999. The location was in Yucca Valley, California. I remember it well. It was a bittersweet story of surrender. At first, you may wonder what it has to do with the crown chakra but stay with me and you will find out.

The experience started in a setting that felt like a palace or a temple of some sort. I was a woman and I noticed that the energy of the people in the streets felt tense. Soon I realized that I was a princess or priestess. Regardless, I was the king's daughter. The king was a tyrant. He was very controlling and ordered all of the slaves to give up their youngest male child. I was appalled; I had to do something to help these people that I had befriended and come to know. As a young girl, I would go into the streets and co-mingle with the lower class.

My plan was to help the people and lead them away from the kingdom. In this experience, I felt myself riding on a camel or a horse and we were traveling in the middle of the night. We found a safe resting place and set up camp. Not too much time went by before the soldiers found us. They didn't hesitate to kill and slaughter all of the people who left the kingdom. I witnessed a massacre and I heard every scream and cry. My body became numb and I was devastated. At that point, I hated my Father.

Upon returning to the kingdom, I quickly drew a tub of water to soak in. My bath always contained essential oils and scents to soothe me. While I was lying and soaking in the tub, I sensed someone enter the room. I already knew who it was and what was going to happen. I didn't care, I was brokenhearted. I blamed myself for the slaughter of the people I tried to help. Just then, my lover, who was also the king's knight, kneeled over me in the fragrant tub and placed his strong, mighty hand on my throat. He pushed me into the deep warm water. I never opened my eyes as the bubbles emerged out of my esophagus—one, two, three—I surrendered.

Having the status of priestess, I was given a proper ceremony for my journey into the spiritual realms. My glowing, gold sarcophagus was placed on top of pedestals for display. The people in this kingdom were sad for my loss. They loved me as much as I loved them. They saw me as their beacon of light in times of despair and turmoil. As night fell across the land, I felt my soul emerge from the sarcophagus and lift up to the sky. Then spontaneously, like a galaxy of stars, these drops of light fell from the sky. They were similar to snowflakes. The sprinkles of light fell towards the people and touched them. They imagined these starlight's to be blessings from their priestess as she thanked them for their love. The experience of light particles falling from the sky was a sign for this culture to remember that they are "spiritual beings living a human life."

Surrendering manifests differently for every one of us. More important is remembering that there is a higher power to surrender to. Stan Grof, in *Psychology of the Future*, says, "The deepest motivating force in the psyche on all the levels of consciousness evolution is to return to the experience of our divinity." Too often, the external conditions of our environment prevent us from realizing

148

this truth. Further, it requires a death of the separate self. The experience of one's divinity through a mystical transcendence, be it a Holotropic session or a profound celestial journey, provides the satisfaction necessary to understand we all originate from the same source. This understanding outweighs any external desire and it can only be experienced within.

After completing Inanna's entire story and aligning with the chakra energy, I noticed it has been easier for me to stay awake and remember this sense of oneness with all beings. As I live each moment, I will always be subject to egoic patterns and human material needs. However, because of a connection to a Divine source, I have a cleansed view. My connection with the Divine—with God, Inanna or Jesus—helps me stay on this clear path.

# Chapter Nine –
# Re-Connect and Remember

*Whatever you have forgotten, you can remember. Whatever you have buried you can unearth. If you are willing to look deep into your own nature, if you are willing to peel away the layers of not-self you have adopted in making your way through the tribulations of life, you will find that your true self is not as far removed as you think.*
*~Meredith Jordan*

Inanna's story represents the essential qualities of human life. She is caring, nurturing and patient when she rescues and tends to the tree. She is strong and courageous by standing her ground and taking responsibility for her city's growth. She is confident and loves passionately; she is not afraid to live her truth. She embraces the darkness and represents a fearless being, one who lives her life with passion and purpose, and one who lives fully and completely.

Inanna participates in the conscious reality of human life. She knows that humans encompass a full spectrum of emotions and behaviors. She symbolically leads others to the path of Divine light and embraces all things as part of the whole. In turn, she is respected and treated by her people with love, honor and reverence.

Popular fictional stories such as the *DaVinci Code* and *The Lost Symbol* suggest there is a trend toward de-mystifying the truth of ancient knowledge. These stories also hint towards secret societies honoring a Divine feminine presence. There are many researchers, such as David Wilcock, who offer evidence to prove there are power driven cults secretly honoring the Divine feminine. The United States of America boasts the Statue of Liberty at its doorway. She stands tall in the forefront and gateway of our modern world, yet her primary significance is overlooked. Her remarkable beauty and stature represents a powerful woman. She is carrying a torch. We are told this statue represents the doorway to freedom but

151

symbolically, it represents the eternal and the path or light of immortality.

The Divine feminine is emerging and she is changing us. We are at the forefront of a huge shift that will ultimately balance the energies of our earth and universe. This evolution will balance the yin/yang energies. There are many viewpoints regarding the prophecy of 2012, most of them are fear based. That is because there are some who do not like this feminine uprising and they will resist it at all costs. It is likely that this evolutionary process will take more death, the death of our masculine selves to encounter more of the feminine. However, if we can embrace and surrender to this shift— this ripple in our collective consciousness—it will be easier to integrate the feminine and masculine convergence that will take place regardless.

### The Spiritual Being Living a Human Life

Inanna is one of the original Goddess' to believe in the creation and potential of human life. She has re-emerged in our psyche to lead humanity as a spiritual teacher. Inanna can help us understand the importance of self-control, self-knowledge and self-reverence through living a strong connection to the Divine. This is necessary for humanity to harmonize and live in balance through this profound shift in consciousness. Inanna embraces the great paradox of humanity with her overflowing love and compassion for all.

Our modern era is changing and we are beginning to recognize that we all have the capacity to be mystics or healers. Perhaps this is what Jesus meant when he said, "The Kingdom of Heaven is within you." It is apparent that more people today are awakening to this truth within themselves. This awareness is trickling into our communities and growing. We can see that this is evident through the increase of people's experiences termed "heart openings" or "spiritual awakenings." We are all spiritual beings whether we recognize ourselves as such or not. We share the same source; the universe, the galaxies, the light and the eternal vibration of God.

152

There is an increase in people experimenting with various forms of spiritual practice. In fact, a recent study of baby boomers resulted in 52% showing motivation to practice yoga for their overall health. Additionally, yoga is one of the fastest growing professions in North America and women are on the forefront as teachers of this widespread cultural practice (Yoga Journal, 2010).

The recent trend of interest in various cultural practices provides a sense of unity within humanity. Recognizing and respecting all traditions and religions should be considered a gift. However, I disagree with any religion or culture that believes they are the only path to Divine presence. Especially those sects that want to kill others to prove this point. My focus and intention is the opposite; I would prefer to understand every culture's creation story. Believing that only one culture or ancient civilization is the path to the Divine is an old way of thinking that stems from ancient times when people weren't exposed to other cultures or tribes. Today, with our massive amount of technological communication, we know there are many religious views and it is time to accept them.

Now is the time for all of us to "wake up" and allow an inevitable transformation to take place. This involves a new world order that encompasses new belief systems—allowing for equality and balance throughout the world. In order for this to spread, we must recognize our own spiritual gifts. We all have these gifts within us and it is up to each one to identify and share them with others. Through identifying with archetypes, symbols and myth, we can develop our spiritual identity and our ability to heal others.

### Buddha, Jesus and Inanna

In the modern world, we are way too caught up in our sense of logic and reason. We miss the essential nature of our being which is to trust in the dynamic ebb and flow of life. The great prophets, mystics and saints did not use logic and reason to follow their life path. The enlightened Buddha is a perfect example of our true exemplary nature.

In his story, Siddhartha leaves the palace, where he is safe and secure and about to be appointed King. He hears a call to step outside the palace and he follows this call. He could not control his innate desire to connect with the outside world and experience compassion for all humankind. He did not want to segregate or differentiate—he wanted to unite.

Our Beloved redeemer Jesus was not thinking logically when he turned himself in to the Roman authorities. He, too, knew there would be a serious consequence, but he didn't resist. In his very last breaths of human life, we hear his voice of wisdom as he speaks his final words, "Father, forgive them, for they know not what they do." Jesus represents to us a human being who has faith in a higher source and trusts in his Fathers wisdom.

Inanna represents a woman who knows her whole Self. She trusts and acknowledge the depths of her inner wisdom. Inanna's story emphasizes two journeys. The first journey is to visit her father Enki, the God of Wisdom, where she eagerly accepts the powers. She must then bypass seven ports. Seven is a sacred, mystical and magical number. It symbolizes cosmic and spiritual order and the completion of a natural cycle (Tresidder, 2000). Inanna completes the cycle and returns home.

In her second journey, she again proves herself as a fearless woman. She must remove all of her personal, prized possessions before she can pass through the seven gates. Inanna surrenders to a call that unwittingly leads her to death. This is the first written story of a deity facing death and being reborn. She is an empowered woman and has supernatural powers beyond our human experience. This journey implies Inanna is an immortal being.

The Spiritual Warrior

In the book *Inanna, Lady of Largest Heart*, Betty Meador suggests to us that we own who we really are. She shares the story of an empowered woman to help us realize this truth. Meador wrote about the high priestess Enheduanna. This priestess, claimed as King Sargon's daughter, is an extraordinary woman who worshiped Inanna. In the 3ʳᵈ millennia BCE, Enheduanna writes down her story. She represents the capacity to think for herself. She is an insightful, passionate poet who lived on the cusp of an enormous cultural shift. It is evident from her poetic writings that she has a close relationship with Inanna. Enheduanna is a confident woman and she is not afraid to express herself. She feels the turmoil within her and expresses anger through her writing.

Enheduanna is connected to both her masculine and feminine energy and embodies healthy aspects of both. In the book, *Inanna: Lady of Largest Heart,* the reader connects with this high priestess and recognizes her inner strength and strong will. She embodies the courage of a spiritual warrior faced with life-threatening challenges. It is obvious that Inanna plays an important role for Enheduanna. Inanna is a powerful leader who does not relent when faced with confrontation. Both she and Enheduanna are spirited sacred activists that face confrontation and stand strong despite serious conflict. They were both instrumental in inspiring their followers to have faith. They were both spiritual warriors in their time.

This is the kind of mindset and attitude women should prepare themselves for. We, too, are in the midst of an enormous cultural shift. The Western woman is beginning to represent strength in troubled times. This attitude will become an important influence for others going through crisis and chaos. A spiritual warrior has balanced feminine and masculine energy. Equally important, a spiritual warrior is not afraid to trust in Divine presence. If a woman is aware of her ego and she is willing to grow, to develop self-knowledge, she will become a great leader.

As a spiritual warrior, it is possible to love all beings, all faiths and all humankind with an understanding that you are part of the One. Based on recent upheavals in the Mideast and recent natural disasters, the world needs a new shift in consciousness so we can unite and help each other in any way possible. This will require a transformation in our hearts, lending compassion for those we don't know and giving as if we are all from the same source. Our future will depend on many people coming together and volunteering to be in service for humanity.

Many of the stories from ancient times, either fact or fiction, include women as an integral part of growth and development. Women have a great capacity to take on major change but they must prepare and empower themselves to do so. This involves taking responsibility for human development and heeding to the call. Women are being called to reconnect and bring light to their feminine Goddess energy.

### Women Taking Responsibility

In the Introduction of this book, I shared an experience of going into an altered state of consciousness and identifying with archetypal realms. I identified with a presence that was below the surface—it was underground. The darkness enveloped me and I heard a voice say, "open the box." I was afraid to open the box, but I eventually surrendered. What emerged was a cloud of purple and my breath was taken away. I was wrapped in this presence and lifted up to the light. It felt joyous, like a coming home or a celebration!

By identifying with the underworld and surrendering to my unconscious, I was given a gift of beauty and light. Ironically, this experience is a good metaphor for what is happening in the world today. If we connect with the darkness within, we may better relate to the upcoming convergence of energies creating a rebirth of consciousness in 2012.

In *Alchemy of Light, Working With the Primal Energies of Life*, Vaughan-Lee emphasizes the importance of creating a relationship with internal forces "without being overwhelmed by their raw power and without being sucked into unconsciousness" (2007). We must listen as the unconscious presents a new way for us.

We have to be willing to "uncurse" the dark, as Betty Meador says, by facing the dark with humility and strength. We must recognize that our feminine nature will inevitably be the catalyst for restoring our natural wholeness. Women are entering a new sanctuary of self-understanding that will grow out of repeated descents into the fertile dark. From this darkness, new cultural forms will take life.

When women are together in large groups, they create a container. This container holds all the possibilities of human life: the strong, the wicked, the injured, the divorced, the tired mother and the spiritual woman—all able to honor each other no matter how beautiful, adorned or ugly and babbling. Women can mirror other women, much like an archetype, by honoring either their conscious or unconscious beliefs.

Betty Meador wrote an article called, *Uncursing the Dark: Restoring the Lost Feminine*, which emphasizes the importance of women taking responsibility, she quotes:

> The feminine images of the self emerging from the unconscious are a call to a new order. Women are being challenged by...ancient images to accept nothing less than a reorientation of the psyche...to a new experience of Inanna's full incarnation. Women are being challenged to stretch themselves beyond the security and familiarity of American cultural roles into a new embrace of dark and light. Women are being asked to invent new cultural forms which will enhance and contain the whole expression of the female Self and to pioneer in the face of stiff opposition outside and their own fears, doubts, and loneliness inside. (1989)

This journal was published twenty years ago. Since then we have been witnessing this transformation of women taking on a whole new outlook in life.

Samuel Noah Kramer devoted his whole life to the Sumerian culture and his last book, co-authored with Diane Wolkstein, was an attempt to lift the veil and bring a new awareness for human growth. In other words, the liberated woman is nothing new—it is very ancient. In

Kramer's autobiography, he states that Inanna is the one Goddess who should serve not only as a soothing balm to the wounds of women but as a powerful model. Her courage, strength and ambition combined with her love and passion for humanity represents a woman of the new millennia.

### My Relationship with Inanna

Having a personal relationship with Inanna has helped me awaken. Identifying with her story has empowered me. In Joseph Campbell's book, *Myths to Live By*, he tells us that "Through a dialogue conducted with these inward forces, through...a study of myths we can learn to know and come to terms with the greater horizon of our own deeper and wiser, inward self" (1972). My deeper, wiser self wants to uncover who I truly am.

There will always be parts of myself that exist in the dark shadows but I am open to knowing what they are and accepting them. I remember the first time I heard of this *shadow* concept, I didn't get it. Fortunately, I stayed open to the concept and woke up to some personality traits that were keeping me from reaching my highest potential. Since identifying with Inanna's stature and empowering presence, I am not afraid to unveil my inner Goddess.

The story of Inanna can serve as a personal handbook for anyone. This book makes her story easy to understand while highlighting the value of our spiritual nature. Inanna's story incorporates the universal laws of nature and the virtues women are born with.

In an article written in 2002, Eloise Hart shares, "Like Inanna, we have but to open our "ears" to find [inner] wisdom and truth." Through awareness of these virtues "we can venture forward forever, leaving our outgrown shells like a corpse hung on a wall...relying upon love and wisdom of the mother/priestess/goddess that we are in our hearts" (Hart, 2002). Inanna helps us identify with these inner feminine qualities we all possess.

Now is the perfect time for Inanna to be revealed and acknowledged in human consciousness. We already

158

see her every day. She is Venus, the bright and beautiful morning and evening star. Through an awakening of the Goddess within, we can prepare for a shift in consciousness. For some, it will be subtle, not even noticeable, for others it may take a huge life event to awaken and align with a new outlook. In either case, it will require balancing the feminine and masculine energy and taking an interest in self-growth.

Women are already taking responsibility for their families and themselves. They are more focused on living healthy and balanced lives. The next step for women will be to connect with this feminine energy on a deeper scale. Identifying with the psycho-spiritual aspects of the chakras is one method to use. This can be taken a step further by practicing Kundalini Yoga. Additionally, the practice of Holotropic Breathwork is another unconventional option to connect with the inner feminine, the unconscious.

Holotropic Breathwork has been a very influential practice for my self-growth. There are many spiritual practices available today to explore. The most important thing to remember is to find the method that resonates with your soul. When seeking to awaken the conscious, it may not always be comfortable, but it must feel safe and right for you. When the process begins you will begin to see life for what it really is.

Carl Jung has argued that it is only through the transformation of consciousness that we can change and grow. He tells us that all the greatest and most important problems of life are fundamentally insoluble. In other words, they can never be solved, only outgrown. This "outgrowing" requires a new level of consciousness and even some higher or wider interest appearing on the horizon (1959). If we are willing to stay present to these levels, be honest with ourselves and believe in the ability to overcome these traits while striving for a better character, we have a good chance of reaching what Abraham Maslow calls our "highest potential."

Maslow believes that the "self-actualizing man is not an ordinary man with something added, but rather the ordinary man with nothing taken away" (1973). He says the average man, on the other hand, is a full human being with dampened and inhibited powers and capacities. In my studies of Transpersonal Psychology, I learned of Maslow's theory and immediately related to this quote: "Self-actualizing people see life clearly...they are less emotional and more objective, less likely to allow hopes, fears, or ego defenses to distort their observations" (1971). To reach a peak or to sustain a healthier level of one's consciousness requires discipline and a willingness to succeed.

In reference to self-growth, Carl Jung said, "it results in a change to the self, opening it inward toward psycho-spiritual self-knowledge and outward toward increased connection with humanity and the desire to be of service" (1906). This is true with any method of self-growth. It should result in a desire to be in service for humanity.

This undoubtedly takes time and a commitment. Trust in your own process. Listen to what is guiding and motivating you to explore more of yourself. Take the time to meditate or pray about something before you jump into it. Pay attention to your motivations and reasons for gaining knowledge whether it is self-knowledge or a new skill. This way you will have a better indication of whether it is really right for you. Even further growth is encouraged as you become aware that your capabilities are not static We go on refining and improving as our life proceeds, returning again and again to revisit our understanding as our spiritual development continues.

People who have done a significant amount of inner work know it is a continuous process. For me, there are days when I welcome working with a clean, polished slate. I am fueled by the idea that this blank slate starts with love. After all, the base of our existence started with a Divine intention to love all things. As life cycles, it is important to let go of fears, embrace all parts of the self and practice a daily discipline that fosters a cleansed view and an ability to see through a compassionate lens.

My hope is that more people will begin to remember this truth and that, with each passing moment, we are able to recognize the love we give, as equally as we recognize the love we receive. Moreover, I hope that people will reach their highest potential and strive toward a deeper connection with an all-knowing, all-embracing Divine presence.

Campbell and Jung both agree that identifying with myth allows us to embrace transformation. This is evident through thousands of years of human stories. Storytelling has been a part of our human nature since before Inanna's story was written. We are fortunate to have this story in writing and have the knowledge to translate it. Let's utilize this ancient myth, this profound feminine archetype, for our own awakening. Let's embrace the Divine feminine once again in an effort to save our world. If we hear the call, we only need to respond, and allow her to lead us in nurturing and caring for humanity and for our beloved Mother Earth.

*...and let it so be said!*

# APPENDIX A:

## HOLOTROPIC BREATHWORK™

In the early 1980's, Stanislav Grof, M.D. and Licensed Psychologist, discovered Holotropic Breathwork. Stan and his wife, Christina, were living at the Esalen Institute in Big Sur, CA, and started working with groups using deeper and faster breathing while listening to a variety of cultural music. Stan and Christina incorporated material from disciplines such as yoga, indigenous shamanic practices, and intense experiential psychotherapies to develop Holotropic Breathwork (Grof, 2000).

The theory and practice of Holotropic Breathwork is based on observations from modern consciousness research. Holotropic literally means, "moving towards wholeness." This method of therapy and self-exploration combines simple means to induce Holotropic states of consciousness—faster breathing, evocative music, and releasing bodywork. The transformative power of these states can be very healing when facilitated properly. The safe setting and support allows people to let go into a Holotropic state.

Holotropic Breathwork begins by lying on a mat on the floor. The person starts the session laying face up or in open *savasana* position. When the music begins the participant starts breathing a little deeper and a little faster. The music is loud and powerful and is made up of a variety of intense cross-cultural music. The intention is to induce an altered or Holotropic state of consciousness. This is an all natural process using the breath to allow an opening or healing in the psyche. A typical session will usually last two to three hours. The Grof's have conducted workshops around the world since the 1980's. Following is a clip from their media and advertisement:

*Holotropic Breathwork is a powerful way of deeply opening to innate healing in our mind, body, and spirit. It permits deep self-exploration, healing, and spiritual opening of the self. This process can bring about awareness and transformation at all levels. Events that occur in our personal history, in the circumstances of our birth, or in transpersonal realms can create constrictions that impede the flow of our creative energy. These constrictions may keep us from attaining the personal wholeness, community feeling and intelligence of spirit that brings fullness and satisfaction to life. We may also feel stress, anxiety, or physical discomforts that conventional medicine cannot relieve. Consequently, we may experience difficulty with our interpersonal relationships and lack a sense of life's purpose. Holotropic Breathwork offers a powerful way to resolve these problems. It motivates us to achieve our full potential by helping us overcome feelings that we are stuck, trapped, blocked, or burdened. "Holotropic" means "turning toward wholeness," that inner capacity for self-healing at the heart of our being that makes healing possible* (2008).

The process of self-exploration and therapy in Holotropic Breathwork is spontaneous and autonomous: it is governed by the inner healing intelligence of the breather, rather than guided by a therapist following the principles of a particular school of psychotherapy.

It is important to mention that entering into a Holotropic state should be done with caution. Caution, in Grof's words is: "Adequate preparation, support, and guidance are critical prerequisites for exploring the deep territories of the human mind" (2006). This caution is one of the key elements in the makeup of a Holotropic Breathwork setting. It is also the central theme in Grof's Transpersonal Training. Fore more information on the training, visit the website www.holotropic.com.

The principal constituents of Holotropic Breathwork are: breathing, instrumental music, bodywork and mandala drawing. Each of these will be explored below in more detail, however, I encourage the reader to visit the Holotropic website or read one of Grof's books.

The material below was selected from the most recent book, *Holotropic Breathwork: A New Approach to Self-Exploration and Therapy* (Grof & Grof, 2010). All of the elements used in Holotropic Breathwork, have been used in sacred practices and native cultures for thousands of years. The healing potential of Holotropic Breathwork represents rediscovery, validation, and modern reformation of ancient wisdom and procedures, some of which can be traced to the dawn of human history.

In ancient and pre-industrial societies, breath and breathing have played a very important role in cosmology, mythology, and philosophy. Since the beginning of time, humans have viewed breath as a crucial link between the material world, the human body, the psyche and spirit (Grof & Grof, 2010). It has been known for centuries that it is possible to influence consciousness by techniques that involve breathing. Some of the modern breathing practices today are: Kundalini Yoga, Siddha Yoga, Sufi practices, Burmese Buddhist and Taoist meditation, among many others.

**Breathing**: Instead of emphasizing a specific technique of breathing during Holotropic Breathwork, the main points are to include a cyclic, continuous breath, to breathe a little deeper and faster, to allow the music to stimulate a rhythm with the breath, and to trust the intrinsic wisdom of the body and follow inner clues. In most cases, this process comes naturally. A very helpful point to remember is to let the egoic mind relax and take a break.

**Instrumental Music**: In Holotropic Breathwork, the consciousness-expanding effect of breath is further enhanced by the use of music. In many cultures, music has been used for healing purposes in the context of intricate ceremonies. Some spiritual traditions have developed sound technologies that not only induce a general trance state, but have a specific effect on consciousness and the body. In India, there are teachings that describe specific connections between certain acoustic frequencies and the individual chakras.

Carefully selected music serves important functions in Holotropic states of consciousness. This helps to open the door into the unconsciousness. It intensifies and deepens the healing process while providing a meaningful context for the experience. The continuous flow of music acts as a wave to help the breather surrender and let go.

**Releasing Bodywork**: In many cases and depending on a breather's situation, no external bodywork or interventions are necessary with Holotropic Breathwork. The deep emotions and physical manifestations that emerge from the unconscious during Holotropic sessions are automatically resolved and the breather ends up in a deeply relaxed meditative state. However, if the breathing, in and of itself, produces residual tensions or unresolved emotions, trained facilitators offer participants a specific form of bodywork.

The general strategy of this work is to ask the breather to focus his or her attention on the area of the body that feels blocked or tense and increase their breathing. This result accentuates the tension in that part of the body. The facilitator then offers pressure on this area and encourages the breather to vocalize their reactions. Additionally, the breather is encouraged to move spontaneously and allow the body to react organically. Before the session begins, the breather is instructed to use the word "stop" to remain in complete control of the situation.

In many situations, supportive and nourishing physical contact is necessary for the breather's session to feel complete. Many people have a history of emotional deprivation, abandonment and neglect. One way to heal this type of trauma is to offer a corrective experience in the form of supportive physical contact in a Holotropic state of consciousness. Use of nourishing physical contact is a very effect way of healing but it requires following strict ethical rules.

**Mandala Drawing or Expressive Art**: Mandala is a Sanskrit name for "circle" or "completion." The mandala is a visual construct that can be easily grasped by the eye as it corresponds to the structure of this organ. In many rituals and spiritual practices, a mandala is an image used for meditation aids. It helps focus attention inside. When used in Holotropic Breathwork, the mandala drawing accentuates the session and captures a "mind's eye" view of the experience. This helps the breather

166

integrate or assimilate the process before sharing their experience in a group setting.

Grof's Cartography of the Mind

Grof has over thirty years of experience and thousands of sessions witnessing individuals undergoing Holotropic or altered states of consciousness. These experiences included not only a variety of emotional and physical sensations but also experiences beyond the physical realms. Grof defines Holotropic as "moving in the direction of wholeness" (1998). He characterizes Holotropic states as a transformation of consciousness associated with perceptual changes in the sensory and emotional thought processes (2000).

Grof's initial view of modern psychology was limited to a postnatal biography and to the Freudian individual unconscious. Grof realized his research and ideas in the conscious realms could not be explained in current academic psychiatry and psychology. He writes, "In the early years of my psychedelic research, I sketched a vastly expanded cartography of the psyche" (2006). This cartography consists of two domains: the perinatal domain and the transpersonal domain. The perinatal domain reflects its close connection to birth and the transpersonal domain is defined as reaching beyond the personal identity.

*The Perinatal Domain:* Grof's perinatal domain includes the Basic Perinatal Matrices. These matrices were subsequently identified through acronyms of BPM I, II, III, and IV. These four categories identify with the birth process and make up the perinatal domain. The word perinatal is a composite of the Greek-Latin prefix *peri* which means "around" or "near" and the root *natalis* signifies "pertaining to birth" (2006).

BPM I corresponds to the oceanic bliss of gestation, BPM II to the beginning of constriction before the birth canal is opened, BPM III to the struggle for survival through the birth canal and BPM IV to the final delivery into the external world. Our physical birth is the "most profound trauma of our life and an event of

167

paramount psychospiritual importance" (Grof, 2006). Sensations surrounding our birth range from life-threatening confinement to a determined struggle to free ourselves and survive. Thus, our birth is essentially a mixture of feelings: feelings that relate to near death experiences and feelings of survival, liberation and freedom.

The memory of birth is of utmost importance when identifying with fears of death. Grof writes, "This explains why the process of psychospiritual death and rebirth can free us from such fear and transform our way of living" (2006). The perinatal domain is rich and complex but offers enormous healing benefits in an individual's psyche.

*The Transpersonal Domain:* The other aspect of Grof's work is the transpersonal domain. This term literally means "reaching beyond the personal" or "transcending the personal" (2000). The transpersonal domain differs from the perinatal domain because it extends beyond our biographical, sensory and physical self. However, Grof has observed that people undergoing profound healing crisis seem to undergo transpersonal journeys that have deep parallels to these different stages of birth. Grof writes:

> The no-exit stage of birth (BPM II) is often associated with images of hell and archetypal figures representing eternal damnation...and with corresponding past-life experiences. Typical experiential concomitants of the struggle through the birth canal are archetypal images of deities representing death and rebirth...the reliving of birth is represented by culture-specific images of the Great Mother Goddess and scenes of divine epiphany or sacred marriage (2000).

The transpersonal domain includes experiences of three large categories. All three categories have the theme of going beyond "our skin encapsulated ego," or beyond space and time but differ in the level of boundaries, or lack of boundaries that are reached. The first category primarily involves transcending the usual spatial barriers. This is most commonly related to identification with another person or culture. It could be identification with plants and animals or oneness with life and all of creation (Grof, 2000). The second category of transpersonal experiences is characterized by overcoming temporal rather than spatial boundaries. This could be transcendence of linear time as in a past life incarnation or ancestral experiences.

The third category is most important for identifying with the Goddess Inanna. Her presence in my Holotropic states opened my psyche and I realized this experience fits with Grof's third category: experiential extension beyond space and time. Grof quotes:

> Here consciousness seems to extend into realms and dimensions that the Western industrial culture does not consider "real," such as numerous visions of archetypal beings and mythological landscapes, encounters with or even identification with deities and demons.....and communication with....spirit guides (2006).

Grof also specifies the various archetypal experiences available: "In its farthest reaches, individual consciousness can identify with cosmic consciousness known under many different names—Brahman, Buddha, Christ...and many others." In my Holotropic experiences, Inanna, Queen of Heaven and Earth, is just one of the archetypes that emerged in my psyche as an archetypal being. I also had reoccurring experiences of direct dialogue with Jesus and various tribal or shamanic healers.

*Grof's Research with LSD*

Grof's exploration of the transpersonal realms was unique (1980). Although his studies were developed from various schools of Depth psychology, his original source was the result of clinical studies working with thousands of patients administering small dosages of LSD for psychoanalytic therapy. The focus of this research was for patients who were dying of cancer. The more familiar changes observed in cancer patients were alleviation of depression, tension and anxiety. These symptoms were also alleviated through traditional forms of therapy (2006). However, Grof discovered there were radical changes in basic life philosophy, such as decreasing or elimination of fear of death that he identified as reaching beyond the confines of modern psychotherapy. The dying cancer patients experienced a psychospiritual death and rebirth from the psychedelic sessions. Grof shares that a profound death-rebirth sequence is a new and powerful mechanism for eliciting therapeutic changes and deep restructuring of the personality (2006).

According to Grof, an experiential confrontation with death via near death experiences (NDE's) also resulted in those people feeling more peaceful. People who have these experiences are left feeling more comfortable with themselves and more tolerant of others. Grof states, "Spirituality also emerges from this process, spirituality of a universal and mystical nature that is very authentic and convincing because it is based on a deep, personal experience." Grof finds an even broader dimension to this process which encompasses the deep humanitarian and ecological concerns that are emerging today. He adds, "Individuals who are able to confront death and come to terms with it in their inner process tend to develop a sense of planetary citizenship, reverence for life in all its forms, deep ecological sensitivity, spirituality of a universal and all-encompassing type" (2000). Through a deep, transformative process one can undergo a complete shift in how they live their life. In today's society, more and more people are willing to search inside of themselves and experience a psychospiritual death and rebirth (Grof, 2000).

## Psychoanalysis, Depth Psychology and Carl Jung

Grof's (2000) concepts and ideas were not altogether new. Although his ideas resulted from LSD research, his concepts "represent a synthesis of the perspectives of various schools of depth psychology known from the history of psychoanalysis" (2006). Depth psychology and psychoanalysis proved to be indicative therapeutic tools for many psychologists in the 1900s. Carl Jung is known worldwide in the field of psychology as a depth psychologist. He is also known for discovering transpersonal realms.

Other early transpersonal thinkers include William James, who focused on higher consciousness, and Robert Assagioli, who studied different spiritual practices for use as a psychotherapeutic tool. Abraham Maslow, one of the founders of humanistic and transpersonal psychology, recognized that individuals can have a "peak experience." A "peak experience" is described by a sense of unity or transcendence of time and space and is comparable to Grof's transpersonal domain (Grof, 2006). Maslow says that when a person has a "peak experience" he or she begins to self-actualize and reach a state of unity or wholeness striving to be in community and in service.

Grof was mostly interested in exploring Jung's work and his theories of the collective unconscious. Although Jung was a supporter of Freudian theory he was an unconventional explorer. He began to suspect that there was more going on in the individual unconscious mind and postnatal biographical memories. The collective unconscious represents a connection in the psyche to symbolic modes of existence (Jung, 1968). These symbolic forces he called archetypes and the place where they existed he called the collective unconscious.

Jung found evidence of a collective unconscious that related to all human beings. By expanding the boundaries of our inner lives, Jung's philosophy was more than therapeutic. "Jung was convinced that through getting a handle on archetypes, those subtle architects of the collective unconscious, we would begin to get a handle on ourselves and our unconscious inner world and discover a more integrated sense of individuality" (Phipps, 2008).

Jung defined an archetype as "ideas in the Platonic sense that perform and influence continually our thoughts and feelings and actions" (Jung, 1968). James Hillman, an eminent Jungian psychologist, described archetypes as the deepest patterns of psychic functioning (1975). Hillman believed the best comparison to an archetype is to a God or Goddess. Hillman and Jung were already speaking about the transpersonal dimensions in their time. Grof recognized Jung's description of these archetypes while facilitating people in Holotropic states. His research and studies proved evidence of transpersonal dimensions. Grof has included various experiences of archetypes in his many books.

# APPENDIX B:

## Kundalini Yoga &
## The Chakra Energy System


### What is Kundalini Yoga?

Most of the information in this appendix about Kundalini Yoga, I took from the book *Kundalini Yoga: The Flow of Eternal Power,* written by an advanced Kundalini Yoga instructor by the name of Khalsa (1996). I have taken many Kundalini Yoga classes myself and will testify it is extremely powerful. However, in my opinion, Holotropic Breathwork is much more powerful due to the internal nature and length of the session. I have had extraordinary experiences in Kundalini Yoga but with no external intention, I did not integrate them or share them with others. Having said that, one is not better than the other rather the two together are a great source for self-growth.

To define Kundalini Yoga, we should define yoga first. Yoga means to be united. When you unite with your soul and unite with the source who gave you the soul, that's what yoga is. Kundalini Yoga basically means, "uncoil yourself." When you do yoga in an involved conscious way and you allow your mind to open to all the possibilities of the conscious mind, this is Kundalini Yoga. Kundalini also means the creative potential of humanity.

For thousands of years this yogic knowledge was carefully handed down by oral tradition from Master to disciple. The Master spoke and the student memorized through practice. Eventually a portion of this vast body of knowledge was written down. Some of these sacred teachings can be found in ancient Vedic texts. Kundalini Yoga was always kept very secret. It was never taught publicly until 1969, when Yogi Bhajan challenged the ages-old tradition of secrecy. He spent many years mastering and perfecting the practices of Kundalini Yoga. He offered to share these ancient secrets with the Western world. His motive was to spread awareness and compassion throughout the world. Yogi Bhajan sees the reality of our inner beauty, power and potential. He wants us to discover it for ourselves.

Kundalini Yoga is not a religion, it is a Sacred Science. It is sacred because it connects us with the Divine. It is scientific because it provides a technology, a method by which anyone who practices it can experience Divinity within. This method is based on postures and a specific series of verbal or sometimes silent words. A typical Kundalini Yoga class would be done in a traditional yoga studio. People who have been doing it a long time sit on a material that is compatible with the flow of energy. There are many postures; some sitting, some lying down, some standing. It varies depending on the *kriya*.

**What Does Kundalini Yoga Do?**

The practice of Kundalini Yoga balances the glandular system, strengthens the nervous system and enables us to harness the energy of the mind and the emotions. This way we are controlling our thoughts instead of our thoughts controlling us. It is a dynamic, powerful tool for expanding awareness.

Kundalini Yoga deals specifically with the most powerful thing in the universe, the *qi* or *prana*, the basic life energy. *Prana* is the sub-atomic energy, the life force. It was known to yogis for thousands of years, long before the scientists split the atom. It is *prana* that you receive with every breath. Kundalini Yoga is the path of discovery of the source of the *prana* in us and teaches us how to use it.

In Kundalini Yoga, the natural flow of energy flowing through the body starts from the root chakra. It begins in the root chakra, is pushed up into the higher chakras to create balance and harmony, and is brought back down to the lower center to be released. Yogi Bhajan speaks of Kundalini: "It is creating the *prana* (life energy) in the cavity and mixing it with *apana* (cleansing energy) and taking it down and again bringing it up. This is Kundalini."

174

The practice of Kundalini Yoga also focuses on the vibration of the body. This is important here because awareness of the energies that lie dormant in this chakra can be both positive and negative. Words of love and compassion, kindness and generosity to all humankind resonate at a higher vibration. The opposite is true of words of anger, jealousy, resentment, egotism and fear. These words pull our energy down into our lower chakras. Khalsa, a student of Yogi Bhajan, says "Your consciousness is exactly, precisely at that place, at any given moment, where your thoughts and words are vibrating" (1996). This goes beyond moral judgment. Now we are speaking about energetic sense and desiring a higher vibration.

Kundalini Yoga is better experienced than understood. At least, it should be experienced if one wants to fully understand it. The best thing to do is search on the internet for a practitioner near you and keep an open mind. It is not the easiest practice but it most certainly reaps big rewards on our overall mind, body, spirit awareness and wholeness of health.

## *The Chakra Energy System*

I ask people all the time if they know about chakras. Some do but usually they nod their head and make a face that tells me they barely do. Typically, if a westerner has heard about the chakras, it is because they are educated about the body's energy system or they heard something about it from a yoga instructor.

Eastern cultures understand the chakra energy system because they learn about it early in life. Eastern medicine is based on the healing and wholeness of the whole body, including the energy. The energy of the body correlates with our development as human beings and blockages can form in the chakras causing various symptoms as well as psycho-spiritual imbalance.

Since ancient times, humans have known and understood the chakras or the energy field. From early Egyptian literature to Native American teaching, there are references to light emanating from the body. In many cultures, there is supporting evidence through imagery. Some examples are: the presence of haloes around the head, the false beard protecting the throat chakra, tiara's, crowns or headgear are all indicators of protection for the brow and crown chakra (Davies, 2000). In this book, Inanna's personal garments are depicted as relating to the chakras.

In today's modern world, we do have evidence of the energy field, yet few recognize it. From my professional perspective, I still wonder why modern science would continue to doubt thousands of years of ancient teachings. The understanding of energy pathways in the organ meridians is the same understanding of the chakras. This is also true for auras and the outer electromagnetic field. The sooner we identify with this energy, the sooner we can relate to our whole body and heal any imbalances.

In each chapter of this book, I already discussed the depth of the psycho-spiritual aspects of the chakras. In this appendix, I include the location of each chakra and the physical location, color and possible physical imbalances which can show up as symptoms in the body.

Keep in mind, this is only a brief summary of each chakra. To learn more and get a broader, more comprehensive approach, I recommend finding a book or website that focuses only on the chakra energy system. I have included a few of my favorite resources at the bottom, if interested.

**ROOT** – Base of spine, coccyx. Color: Red.
One word description: Survival
Imbalances: Anemia, fatigue, lower back pain, sciatica, depression. Frequent colds or cold hands and feet.

**SACRAL** – Below navel, lower abdomen. Color: Orange
One word description: Feelings
Imbalances: Addictions from eating disorders or Alcohol and drug-abuse. Depression. Low back pain. Asthma or allergies. Candida & yeast infections. Urinary problems. Sensuality or sexuality issues as well as impotency or frigidity.

**SOLAR PLEXUS** – Above the navel, stomach area.
Color: Yellow   One word description: Power
Imbalances: Digestive problems, ulcers, diabetes,
hypoglycemia, constipation, nervousness, toxicity,
parasites, colitis, poor memory.

**HEART** – Center of Heart.   Color: Green
One word description: Love
Imbalances: Heart and breathing disorders. Heart and
breast cancer. Chest pain. High blood pressure. Passivity.
Immune system problems. Muscular tension.

**THROAT** – Throat region.   Color: Blue
One word description: Communicate
Imbalances: Thyroid imbalances. Swollen glands. Fevers
and flu. Infections. Mouth, jaw, tongue, neck and shoulder
problems. Hyperactivity. Hormonal disorders such as
PMS, mood swings, bloating and menopause.

**BROW** – Forehead, between eyebrows. Color: Indigo
One word description: Vision
Imbalances: Learning disabilities, co-ordination problems,
sleep disorders.

**CROWN** – Top of head.   Color: Violet
One word description: Connected
Imbalances: Headaches, photosensitivity. Mental illness.
Neuralgia. Senility. Right/left brain disorders and
coordination problems. Epilepsy. Varicose veins and blood
vessel problems. Skin Rashes.

*RESOURCES:*

The 7 Healing Chakras written by Brenda Davies, 2000

www.pavanguru.com/chakras

www.chakraenergy.com

# Bibliography

Baring, A. & Cashford, J. (1993), *The myth of the goddess: Evolution of an image.* New York: Penguin Books.

Black, C. (2000), *Our world, our time.* Hillsboro, Oregon: Beyond Words Publishing, Inc.

Bolen, J.S. (1984), *Goddesses in everywoman*, New York: Harper & Row Publishers, Inc.

Campbell, J. (1949), *The hero with a thousand faces.* Princeton University Press, Princeton, New Jersey.

Campbell, J. (1970), *Myths, dreams, & religion: eleven visions of connection.* MJF Books: New York.

Campbell, J. (1972), *Myths to live by:* The impact of science on myth, New York: Penguin Books.

Campbell. J. (1986), *The inner reaches of outer space: Metaphor as myth and as religion.* Novato, CA: New World Library

Cohen, A. (2008). Peace is not the answer. *What is enlightenment?* Issue 39. Lenox, MA: EnlightenNext

Davies, B. (2000), *The 7 Healing Chakras: Unlocking your body's energy centers.* Berkeley, CA: Ulysses Press.

Davies, D. J. (2002). *Death, ritual and belief: the rhetoric of funerary rites.* (2nd Ed.)      New York, Continuum.

Dwyer, W. W. (1992). *Real magic: Creating miracles in everyday life.* New York: HarperCollins Publishers, Inc.

Dunne, C. (1989), *Behold woman: A Jungian approach to feminist theology*, Wilmette, IL: Chiron Publications.

Easwarean E. (2007). *The Dhammapada.* (2nd Ed.) Berkeley, CA: Nilgiri Press.

Eden, D. (2008). *Energy medicine for women: Aligning your body's energies to boost your health and vitality,* New York: Penguin Books.

Estes, C. P. (1992), *Women who run with wolves: Myths and stories of the wild woman archetype.* New York: Ballantine Books.

Feinstein, T. (1997), *Inanna of tiamat.* Ambridge, PA: Taproot Press.

179

Fillmore, C. (1931), *The metaphysical bible dictionary*, Unity
Village, MS: Unity House.

Frymer-Kensky, T. (1992), *In the wake of the goddesses:
women, culture and the biblical transformation of pagan myth*,
New York: Ballantine Books.

Gallagher, A. (2002), *Way of the goddess*, Hammersmith,
London: Thorsons.

Gennep, A. van. (1960). *The rites of passage*. Chicago: The
University of Chicago Press.

Goodall, J. (2004), *The sacred tree*, Twin Lakes, WI: Lotus Press

Grof, S. (1980). *LSD psychotherapy: Exploring the frontiers of the
human mind*. Albany, NY: State University of New York Press.

Grof, S. (1985). *Beyond the brain: Birth, death and
transcendence in psychotherapy*. Albany, NY: State University of
New York Press.

Grof, S. (1998). *The cosmic game: Explorations of the
frontiers of human consciousness*. Albany, NY: State
University of New York Press.

Grof, S. (2000). *Psychology of the future: Lessons from modern
consciousness research*. Albany, NY: State University of New
York Press.

Grof, S. (2006), *When the impossible happens: Adventures in
non-ordinary realities,* Boulder, CO: Sounds True, Inc.

Grof, S. (2007). *The ultimate journey: Consciousness and the
mystery of death*. Saline, MI: McNaughton & Gunn Publishers.

Grof, S. & Grof, C. (2010). *Holotropic breathwork: a new
approach to self-exploration and therapy*. Albany, NY: State
University of New York Press.

Hart, E. (2002), Inanna, Queen of Heaven and Earth. *Sunrise
Magazine, Oct/Nov, 2002*. Pasadena, CA: Theosophical
University Press.

Herder, (1993), *The herder dictionary of symbols*, Wilmette, IL:
Chiron Publications.

Hillman, J. (1975). Archetypal theory. *Loose ends*. Zurich:
Spring Publications.

James, W. (1961). *The varieties of religious experience*. New
York: New American Library.

180

Johnson, R. A. (1993), *The fisher king and the handless maiden: understanding the wounded feeling function in masculine and feminine psychology*, New York, NY: Harper Collins Publishers.

Jung, C. G. (1933). *Modern man in search of a soul*. New York: Harcourt Brace.

Jung, C.G. (1938). *Psychology and religion*. In CW 11: Psychology and Religion: West and East.

Jung, C. G. (1956). Symbols of transformation. *Collected Works of C. G. Jung*. Vol. 5, Bollingen Series XX. Princeton, New Jersey: Princeton University Press.

Jung, C. G. (1961). *Memories, dreams, reflections*. New York: Pantheon.

Jung, C. G. (1968). *The archetypes and the collective unconscious*. Princeton, New Jersey: Princeton University Press.

Jung, C. G. (1996), *The psychology of kundalini yoga: notes of the seminar given in 1932*, Princeton, NJ: Princeton University Press.

Khalsa, S.P.W. (1996), *Kundalini yoga: the flow of eternal power*. New York: The Berkee Publishing Group.

Koltuv, B.B. (1986), *The book of Lilith*, Lake Worth, FL: Nicholas-Hays, Inc.

Kramer, S.N. (1961), *Sumerian mythology: a study of spiritual and literary achievement in the third millennium B.C.* New York: Harper & Row Publishers, Inc.

Kramer, S. N. (1963), *The Sumerians: Their history, culture and character*. Chicago: The University of Chicago Press.

Kramer, S.N. (1979), *From the poetry of sumer: Creation, Glorification, Adoration*, London: University of California Press.

Kramer, S. N. (1988), *In the World of Sumer: An autobiography*. Detroit, MI: Wayne State University Press.

Lajoie, D. H. & Shapiro, S. I. (1992). *Definitions of transpersonal psychology: The first twenty-three years*. Journal of Transpersonal Psychology, Vol. 24.

Leadbeater, C.W. (1987). *The chakras. Wheaton, IL:* Theosophical Publishing House.

Leloup, J. (2002). *The gospel of Mary Magdalene*. Rochester, VT:

181

Inner Traditions International.

Maslow, A. H. (1968). *Toward a psychology of being*. New York:
    Van Nostrand.

Meador, B. (1989), Uncursing the dark; Restoring the lost
    feminine, *Quadrant: the journal of G.G. Jung foundation for
    analytical psychology*, 22 (1), 27-38.

Meador, B. (2000). *Inanna, lady of largest heart*. Austin, TX:
    University of Texas Press.

Moody, R. (1975). *Life after life*. New York: Bantam Books.

Myss, C. (1996), *Anatomy of the spirit: The seven stages of
    power and healing*, New York, NY: Three Rivers Press.

Oppenheim, A.L. (1964), *Ancient Mesopotamia: Portrait of a dead
    civilization*. Chicago, University of Chicago Press.

Pagels, E. (1979). *The gnostic gospels*. New York City: Random
    House

Palmer, P. J. (2000). *Let your life speak: Listening to the voice of
    vocation*. San Francisco, CA: Jossey-Bass Publishers.

Perera, S. B. (1932), *Descent to the goddess: a way of initiation
    for women*, Toronto, Canada: Inner City Books.

Phipps, C. (2008). The cosmos, the psyche & you. *What is
    enlightenment?* Issue 39. Lenox, MA: EnlightenNext.

Rank, O. (1952). *The trauma of birth*. New York: Random House.

Tresidder, J. (2000), *Symbols and their meanings*, London:
    Duncan Baird Publishers.

Vaughan-Lee, L. (1998), *Catching the thread: Sufism, dreamwork &
    Jungian psychology*. Inverness, CA: The Golden Sufi Center.

Vaughan-Lee, L. (2007), *Alchemy of light: working with the
    primal energies of life*, Inverness, CA: The Golden Sufi Center.

Wauters, A. (1997), *Chakras and their archetypes: uniting
    energy awareness and spiritual growth*, Berkeley, CA: Crossing
    Press.

Walker, C.B.F. (1987), *Cuneiform: reading the past*. Los Angeles, CA:
    The Trustees of the British Museum.

Walsh, R. & Vaughan, F. (1993). On transpersonal definitions. *Journal of Transpersonal Psychology*, 25 (2), 125-182.

Wolkstein, D. & Kramer, S.N. (1983). *Inanna: queen of heaven and earth*. New York: Harper & Row Publishers, Inc.

## ABOUT THE AUTHOR

Dr. Karen Castle, MA is a medical intuitive and a holistic healthcare practitioner. As a Dr. of Chinese Medicine, Karen practices this healing medicine through acupuncture, herbs and bodywork. She is Board Certified as a Licensed Acupuncturist in the state of Florida.

Her focus as a healing practitioner is to help people not only feel better but to better understand the complex nature of the human body. Karen feels this encompasses more than just our physical body; it is our energetic and spiritual nature as well.

Karen lives near St Petersburg, FL. She leads a variety of workshops throughout the year. Based on her background and education in Transpersonal Psychology, along with her certification in Holotropic Breathwork™, she leads people in altered states of consciousness to better connect with the whole self. Karen also enjoys educating others on the transpersonal realms and holding space for people to be together in a like-mind environment.

Karen has committed to be in service for humanity which has evolved from her experiences in Holotropic Breathwork. She believes this work has changed her life and she wants to offer this transformative opportunity to others who are willing to take a risk to dive deep into their psyche.

For more information, or to view her website, go to www.karencastle.com.

16036902R00105

Made in the USA
Charleston, SC
02 December 2012